3rd Edition

Legal Will Kit

(United States Edition)

by Enodare Publishing

Bibliographic Data

- International Standard Book Number (ISBN): 978-1-906144-97-5
- Printed in the United States of America
- First Edition: December 2010
- Third Edition: September 2016

Published by:

Enodare Limited
Unit 102
The Northumberlands
Lower Mount Street
Dublin 2
Ireland

Printed and distributed by:

CasmateIPM
22841 Quicksilver Drive
Dulles, VA 20166
United States of America

For more information, e-mail books@enodare.com.

Trademarks

All terms mentioned in this kit that are known to be trademarks or service marks have been appropriately capitalized. Use of a term in this kit should not be regarded as affecting the validity of any trademark or service mark.

Patents

No patent liability is assumed with respect to the use of the information contained herein.

Warning and Disclaimer

Although precautions have been taken in the preparation of this kit, neither the publisher nor the author assumes any responsibility for errors or omissions. No warranty of fitness is implied. The information is provided on an "as is" basis. The author and the publisher shall have neither liability nor responsibility to any person or entity with respect to any loss or damages (whether arising by negligence or otherwise) arising from the use of or reliance on the information contained in this kit or from the use of the forms or documents accompanying it.

IMPORTANT NOTE

This kit is meant as a general guide to preparing your own last will & testament. While considerable effort has been made to make this kit as complete and accurate as possible, laws and their interpretation are constantly changing. As such, you are advised to update this information with your own research and/or advice and to consult with your personal legal, financial and tax advisors before acting on any information contained in this kit.

The purpose of this kit is to educate and entertain. It is not meant to provide legal, financial or tax advice or to create any lawyer-client or advisory relationship. The authors and publisher shall have neither liability (whether in negligence or otherwise) nor responsibility to any person or entity with respect to any loss or damage caused or alleged to be caused directly or indirectly by the information or forms contained in this kit or the use of that information or those forms.

ABOUT ENODARE

Enodare, the international self-help legal publisher, was founded in 2000 by a team including a qualified lawyer. Its aim was simple - to provide access to quality legal information and products at an affordable price.

Enodare's Will Writer software was first published in that year and, following its adaptation to cater for the legal systems of over 30 countries worldwide, quickly drew in excess of 40,000 visitors per month to our website. From this humble start, Enodare has quickly grown to become a leading international estate planning and asset protection self-help publisher with legal titles in the United States, Canada, Australia, the United Kingdom and Ireland.

Our publications provide customers with the confidence and knowledge to help them deal with everyday estate planning issues such as the preparation of a last will and testament, a power of attorney, a living will, administering an estate and much more.

By providing customers with much needed information and forms, we enable them to protect both themselves and their families through the use of easy to read legal documents and forward planning techniques.

The Future….

We are always seeking to expand and improve the products and services we offer. However, in order to do this, we need to hear from interested authors and to receive feedback from our customers.

If something isn't clear to you in our publications, please let us know and we'll try to make it clearer in the next edition. If you can't find the answer you want and have a suggestion for an addition to our range, we'll happily look at that too.

USING SELF-HELP KITS

Before using a self-help kit, you need to carefully consider the advantages and disadvantages of doing so – particularly where the subject matter is of a legal or tax related nature.

In writing our self-help kits, we try to provide readers with an overview of the laws in a specific area, as well as some sample documents. While this overview is often general in nature, it provides a good starting point for those wishing to carry out a more detailed review of a topic.

However, unlike a lawyer advising a client, we cannot cover every conceivable eventuality that might affect our readers. Within the intended scope of this kit, we can only cover the principal areas in a given topic, and even where we cover these areas, we can still only do so to a moderate extent. To do otherwise would result in the writing of a text book which would be capable of use by legal professionals. This is not what we do.

We try to present useful information and documents that can be used by an average reader with little or no legal knowledge. While our sample documents can be used in the vast majority of cases, everybody's personal circumstances are different. As such, they may not be suitable for everyone. You may have personal circumstances which might impact the effectiveness of these documents or even your desire to use them. The reality is that without engaging a lawyer to review your personal circumstances, this risk will always exist. It's for this very reason that you need to consider whether the cost of using a do-it-yourself legal document outweighs the risk that there may be something special about your particular circumstances which might not be taken into account by the sample documents attached to this kit (or indeed any other sample documents).

It goes without saying (we hope) that if you are in any doubt as to whether the documents in this kit are suitable for use in your particular circumstances, you should contact a suitably qualified lawyer for advice before using them. Remember the decision to use these documents is yours! We are not advising you in any respect.

In using this kit, you should also take into account the fact that this kit has been written with the purpose of providing a general overview of the laws in the United States. As such, it does not attempt to cover all of the various procedural nuances and specific requirements that may apply from state to state – although we do point some of these out along the way. Rather, in our kit, we try to provide forms which give a fair example of the type of forms which are commonly used in most states. Nevertheless, it remains possible that your state may have specific requirements which have not been taken into account in our forms.

Another thing that you should remember is that the law changes – thousands of new laws are brought into force every day and, by the same token, thousands are repealed or amended every day! As such, it is possible that while you are reading this kit, the law might well have been changed. Let's hope it hasn't but the chance does exist! Needless to say, we take regular steps (including e-mail alerts) to update our customers about any changes to the law. We also ensure that our books are reviewed and revised regularly to take account of these changes.

Anyway, assuming that all of the above is acceptable to you, let's move on to exploring the topic at hand legal wills.

TABLE OF CONTENTS

INTRODUCTION TO WILLS

Introduction

In this kit, we will give you a brief introduction to wills as well as the laws relating to wills in the United States. After we've done that, we'll take you step-by-step through the process of making your own will. If you already have a firm understanding of wills, you can skip straight to the section and making your will – although we do recommend that you read the information in this kit first before making your will.

What Is a Will?

Simply put, a will is a legal document that allows you to express your desires and intentions regarding the distribution of your property following your death. It is your will that sets out how, when and even why you want your property apportioned between your relatives, friends and charities when you die. As the author of your will, you will be known as the 'testator' if you are male and as the 'testatrix' if you are female. Although the term executor is often used interchangeably.

Types of Wills

There are numerous different types of wills currently in use today. Some are recognized as legal (in certain states), while others are not. You should check with your attorney or state law to see which type of will is valid in your state.

The principal types of wills include:

Simple Wills

This is the most common type of will and usually only provides for the distribution of an estate; the appointment of an executor; and, if required, the appointment of guardians for minor children.

Testamentary Trust Wills

This is a will that provides for the establishment of a trust upon the death of the testator. On the testator's death, certain or all of his or her assets will be transferred into a trust which will thereafter be administered by trustees appointed under the will in accordance with the terms of the will. This type of trust is often used to provide for a spouse or young children.

Pour-Over Wills

A pour-over will is most commonly used with trusts, such as living trusts. It is designed to transfer some or all of the testator's assets to a trust fund following his or her death. The trust fund, in turn, will provide for the management and/or distribution of those assets. Unlike testamentary trust wills, these trusts are not created upon the testator's death, nor are their terms contained within the will document itself. Rather, these trusts are created before the testator dies under a separate trust deed or agreement. The most common example of a trust of this type is a living trust.

Self-Proving Wills

In the normal course, a will is presented to the probate court as part of the probate process. If there is any doubt as to the authenticity of the signature of the testator appearing on a will, the court may call upon the persons who witnessed the execution of the will to certify in court that the signature of the testator appearing on the will is in fact authentic and that the will was validly executed. One way of avoiding having to call these witnesses to court is to pre-validate the testator's signature. To do this, both the testator and the witnesses sign a document called an 'affidavit'. This is little more than a document in which the witnesses acknowledge that they witnessed the testator sign the will. However, the big difference is that it is signed in the presence of a notary who, in turn, officially seals the document to give it authenticity. The court will normally accept the execution of a will with an accompanying affidavit as genuine. The affidavit, when attached to the related will, is generally called a 'self-proving will'.

Holographic Wills

This is a will that has been written in the testator's own hand writing but, unlike most other wills, does not need to be witnessed. This type of will is not valid in every state and we generally recommend that you avoid using such types of will where possible.

Oral Wills (also called nuncupative wills)

As the name suggests, this is a will that is verbally spoken rather than written down on paper. Very few states recognize the validity of such wills and those that do only permit an oral will where it is made during a final illness and in respect of personal property which has a relatively low monetary value.

Joint Wills

A joint will is a single document incorporating the instructions of two people, usually spouses, who dispose of their estates to each other upon the death of either one of them. The will also stipulates what will happen with those assets when the second person dies. A joint will places enormous restrictions on the ability of the surviving person to change his or her mind about how or to whom the assets will pass upon his or her death. As such, we do not recommend the use of joint wills and suggest the use of two separate wills in their place.

Mirror Wills

A mirror will is created when a husband and wife or two partners each make almost identical wills each leaving, for example, everything to each other should they die; and if both partners die together then to named beneficiaries. Unlike joint wills, mirror wills are made on two separate documents and, as such, the parties are free to change the terms of their will as they wish.

Living Wills

Despite its name, this really isn't a will in the normal sense. For example, unlike normal wills, which come into effect or speak from the date of death of the author, a living will applies while the author is still alive. Even more different is its function. While normal wills tend to dispose of property, the effect of a living will is to let doctors and hospitals know whether the author wishes to receive life sustaining medical treatment in the event that he or she is terminally ill or, as a result of accident or illness, in a state of permanent unconsciousness. Living wills, in varying degrees, are valid in all US states.

Why Make a Will?

There are many benefits to making a will and very few drawbacks. Perhaps the biggest benefit is that it allows you to dictate, via a clear legal document, how you want your assets distributed following your death. This is particularly important if you are married or have children as, in each case, you will no doubt want to provide appropriately for your loved ones. In the absence of having a will, the 'rules of intestacy' (which apply where a person dies without making a will) will determine how your assets are distributed amongst your heirs. As the definition of 'heirs' only includes family members, this distribution may not be in accordance with your wishes!

Did You Know

Over 2.6 million Americans die every year (Source: National Vital Statistics Report). Of this number, research by Rocketlawyer indicates that almost 64% haven't made a will and, of those that have made a will (being the other 36%), 12% of those people end up with invalid wills. Therefore a total of approximately 76% of Americans die annually without a valid will.

Another good reason for making a will is that it allows you to appoint someone as your executor. Your executor is the person or persons who will be responsible for carrying out the instructions in your will and for tidying up your affairs after you die. If you don't appoint an executor in your will, the rules of intestacy will determine who fulfils that role. The person appointed under these rules may not be someone that you would wish to have trawling through your affairs.

Wills also allow you to appoint guardians to take care of your minor children and to make property management arrangements to cater for young beneficiaries who will inherit under your will. We'll discuss guardians and property management in more detail in the ensuing pages.

Intestacy & What Happens Without a Will?

When a person dies without making a will or if their will cannot be located, is deemed false or invalid (for not meeting the statutory requirements described below), it's called dying intestate. Each state has a set of statutory rules governing who is entitled to receive a person's property if they die intestate in that state. These rules are commonly known as the 'rules of intestacy' or the 'rules of intestate succession'.

Quite often, the application of the rules of intestacy result in the distribution of a deceased person's property in a manner that they would never have wanted. This is because the rules set out a list of people (known as 'heirs') who are entitled to receive shares in the deceased's property; as well as the amount of these shares and the order in which they are entitled to receive them.

In an intestacy situation, the first beneficiaries to receive the deceased's property are usually the surviving spouse and then the children of the deceased. However, if there is no surviving spouse or children, then the general rule of thumb is that the bigger the estate is, the more distant the relatives who will inherit part of it. Such beneficiaries might include the deceased's grandchildren, parents, siblings, grandparents, nieces and nephews, cousins and so on. In those rare cases where no relatives can be found the deceased's property will revert to the state government's treasury.

 Did You Know

Your estate is the total sum of your possessions, property and money held in your name (minus debts) at the time of your death.

While intestacy laws generally vary from state to state, this variance has been greatly lessened by the Uniform Probate Code ("Code") which, at the time of this writing, has been adopted by 18 states in full and by numerous states in part. The Code is a good place to begin a general discussion on the topic of intestacy. However, you must check your own state law for a more sophisticated and thorough understanding of the Code. The law that usually applies is the state law of your domicile, or principal place residence.

UNIFORM PROBATE CODE - FULL STATE ADOPTIONS

Alaska	Michigan	North Dakota
Arizona	Minnesota	Pennsylvania
Colorado	Montana	South Carolina
Hawaii	Nebraska	South Dakota
Idaho	New Jersey	Utah
Maine	New Mexico	Wisconsin

Under the Code, priority of inheritance is given to the following persons in the following order:

- surviving spouse;

- descendents (children, grandchildren, etc.);

- parents;

- descendents of the deceased's parents (siblings, nieces and nephews);

- grandparents; and

- descendents of grandparents (aunts, uncles and cousins).

Under the Code, relatives are each apportioned a certain percentage of the deceased's estate. The percentages are as follows:

Share of Surviving Spouse

The share of a surviving spouse is calculated as follows:-

- A surviving spouse is entitled to the entire estate if neither the deceased's descendants (i.e. children, grandchildren and great grandchildren) nor the deceased's parents have survived the deceased.

- If the deceased's parents survive but no descendents survive the deceased, the surviving spouse is entitled to the first $200,000 of the estate plus ¾ of anything exceeding that amount.

- If the deceased is survived by a spouse and descendants from that marriage only, the surviving spouse will take the first $150,000 of the estate plus ½ of anything exceeding that amount, plus all community property.

- If the deceased is survived by descendents from the marriage to the surviving spouse and by descendents from someone other than his or her surviving spouse, the surviving spouse takes the first $100,000 of the estate plus ½ of anything exceeding that amount, plus all community property.

Share of Descendents

- If the deceased's spouse does not survive the deceased and the deceased's descendants do, then the deceased's descendents take the entire estate.

- In some cases, if the deceased's child has predeceased the deceased, that child's surviving children will inherit their parent's share of the intestate estate. This is known as 'per stirpes' distribution.

Share of Parents

- If the deceased is not survived by a spouse or descendents, his or her entire net estate passes to his or her parents equally or, if only one survives, to the survivor.

Share of Other Relatives

- If neither the deceased's spouse, descendents, nor parents survive the deceased, the entire net estate passes to the deceased's siblings. If there are no siblings or no descendents of the deceased's siblings, the deceased's estate goes to any surviving grandparents or their descendents.

Even with all these intestacy provisions, if the deceased dies without a will and without traceable relatives or relatives that fall within the scope of the Code or state intestacy provisions, the ultimate successor will be the state treasury!

Partial Intestacy

In addition to providing for situations where a person has died without making a will, the rules of intestacy also apply to situations where a person has failed to deal with all of their property under the terms of their will. This is called a "partial intestacy". Partial intestacy commonly occurs where a will fails to include what's known as a residuary clause. A residuary clause simply provides that any of the deceased's property which has not been specifically gifted to someone under the terms of their will is to be given to a named beneficiary or beneficiaries known as the residuary beneficiary/beneficiaries. A partial intestacy can also occur where the residuary beneficiary or beneficiaries die before the testator and no alternate beneficiaries are named to receive the residue of the estate in their place. Where a partial intestacy occurs, any property not covered under the will shall be distributed in accordance with the rules of intestacy outlined above.

Appointment of Guardians by the Court

Any parent who has parental responsibility for their child should consider appointing a guardian to look after their children in the event that they (and their spouse if married) are unable to do so – through death or otherwise. There are two primary ways of appointing a guardian. Firstly, a formal guardianship agreement can be signed between the parent and the prospective guardian that formally provides for the guardianship arrangement. Alternatively, a clause can be inserted in a will appointing a guardian for the testator's children. This latter method is much more common than the former.

However, if you fail to utilize either of the above methods, you will be unable to appoint a guardian to care for any minor children that you might leave behind following your death. The decision as to who will act as the guardian of your children will be determined in accordance with state laws. The court will usually appoint a relative or other person as guardian of the children depending on what it considers to be in the best interest of the children. This may or may not be someone that you would have approved of.

Appointment of Administrator by the Court

Finally, where you fail to make a will, the rules of intestacy will also determine who will act as the administrator of your estate. The administrator of your estate performs a similar function to an executor. The person appointed will usually be a family member. However, it may or may not be someone that you would have approved of. In fact, it could even be a creditor of your estate if no family member was willing to carry out the task!

It may also be necessary for the administrator to take out an 'administrator bond'. This is a type of insurance bond which is taken out to compensate the estate in the event that its value is depleted due to mismanagement by the administrator. Where such a bond is taken out, the cost will be payable by your estate. This will reduce the value of your overall estate which will pass to your heirs.

Can I Make My Own Will?

Absolutely! Provided your estate is not too complex (and most estates are not complex) and you are <u>not actively trying to disinherit your spouse</u>, you can easily make your own will. While many lawyers will correctly tell you that it's important to get proper legal advice when making a will, the reality is that most of them use simple template or precedent will forms for the vast majority of their clients. These are the same type of templates that are included with this kit. It most cases, all you need to do to prepare your own will is to decide on a few simple matters like who you want to gift your property to, who you want to act as your executor, who you want to act as guardian of your children and who you want to act as witnesses to the execution of your will.

However, when making your will, you should pay close attention to the rights of spouses which will be discussed below. In this respect, if you wish to disinherit them in any manner, you should speak to a lawyer. Similarly, if your estate is large or complex (such as where you own a business or have large agricultural holdings) you should obtain legal and tax advice.

How to Make a Valid Will

Each state has laws which set out the minimum requirements for a conventional will to be valid in that state. In general, in order for a will to be valid, it must:

- be made by a person who has reached the age of majority in their state;
- be made by a person voluntarily and without pressure from any other person;
- be made by a person who is of 'sound and disposing mind';
- be in writing;
- be signed by the testator in the presence of at least two witnesses (three witnesses are required in Vermont);
- be signed by the witnesses in the presence of the testator (after he or she has signed it) and in the presence of each other. A beneficiary under the will or the spouse or registered civil partner of such a beneficiary should not act as a witness to the signing of the will. If they do, the gift to the beneficiary under the will shall be deemed to be invalid, although the will itself will remain valid; and
- include an attestation (signing) clause.

If the above requirements are not complied with, the will may be deemed to be invalid in which case the rules of intestacy will apply.

Age of Majority

The age of majority is a legal description that denotes the threshold age at which a person ceases to be a minor and subsequently becomes legally responsible for his or her own actions and decisions. It is the age at which the responsibility of the minor's parents or guardians over them is relinquished. Reaching the age of majority also has a number of important practical consequences for the minor. The minor is now legally entitled to do certain things which he or she could not legally do before. For example, he or she is now legally entitled to enter into binding contracts, hold significant assets (including inheritances), buy stocks and shares, vote in elections, buy and/or consume alcohol, and so on. But more importantly from an estate planning perspective, the minor can now make a will and a codicil.

The chart below demonstrates the age of majority as defined by each state.

Age of Majority in U.S.	
Age 18	Alaska, Arizona, California, Colorado, Connecticut, District of Columbia, Florida, Georgia, Hawaii, Idaho, Illinois, Indiana, Iowa, Kansas, Kentucky, Louisiana, Maine, Maryland, Massachusetts, Michigan, Minnesota, Missouri, Montana, New Hampshire, New Mexico, New Jersey, New York, North Carolina, North Dakota, Oklahoma, Oregon, Pennsylvania, Rhode Island, South Carolina, South Dakota, Texas, Vermont, Washington, West Virginia and Wyoming.
Age 19	Alabama, Delaware and Nebraska.
Age 21	Mississippi.
Graduation or 18 - (whichever occurs first)	Ohio and Utah.
Graduation or 18 –(whichever occurs later)	Arkansas, Tennessee and Virginia.
Graduation or 18 – (whichever occurs first) or 19 if still at school	Nevada and Wisconsin.

It is a general rule that a person must reach the age of majority in their state before being entitled to make a valid legal will or codicil. There are however some exceptions to this general rule. Typically, a person under the age of majority who is already married, or who has been married, is deemed of sufficient age to execute a will or a codicil. Similarly, an underage person who joins the military or is on active military service can also make a will or a codicil, as can a seaman or naval officer at sea.

Mental Capacity and Undue Influence

In order to make a valid legal will, you must typically be of 'sound disposing mind'. 'Sound disposing mind' is generally taken to mean someone who understands:

- what a will is;

- that they are making a will;

- the general extent of their property;

- who their heirs and family members are; and

- the way in which their will proposes to distribute their property (and, of course, to be satisfied with that.)

It is important to note that you need to be of sound disposing mind when you execute your will, not immediately prior to your death. As such, if you end up suffering from any kind of mental impairment late in life such as dementia or Alzheimer's disease, or even from an addiction to drugs or alcohol, the court will look at your mental state at the time you executed your will in order to determine whether it was validly made. If it can be shown that you were not mentally impaired or under the influence at the time you executed your will, the court will most likely deem the will to be valid. If you are suffering from any such impairments, it is advisable that you visit your doctor on the day you execute your will (or even execute it in your doctor's presence) and have your doctor prepare a medical certificate stating that in his or her professional opinion you were mentally competent and lucid at the time you executed your will. These types of statements generally have a strong persuasive effect on the courts, which typically tend to concede mental lucidity in such cases.

Another form of mental incapacity comes under the heading 'undue influence'. Undue influence is the exertion by a third party in a position of trust or authority of any kind of control or influence over another person such that the other person signs a contract or other legal instrument (such as a mortgage or deed) which, absent the influence of the third party, he or she would not ordinarily have signed. A contract or legal instrument may be set aside as being non-binding on any party who signs it while under undue influence.

Claims of undue influence are often raised by sibling beneficiaries in circumstances where one sibling is bequeathed more from a parent than the others. In making your will, you must therefore be careful to avoid potential claims of undue influence where you leave more to one of your children than another. Any such suggestion would give an aggrieved beneficiary the opportunity to attack and try to overturn the terms of your will. In order to reduce the potential likelihood of such claims, it's often useful to document the reasons why you are leaving more to one child than another. Your note can then be attached to your will or at least kept with it.

A second scenario in which claims for undue influence are often raised arises where a testator uses a beneficiary's lawyer to draft their will. In such circumstances, aggrieved beneficiaries will, in reliance on that very fact, often assert that the use of the beneficiary's lawyer was evidence of the control the beneficiary had over the testator and the pressure that the beneficiary put on the testator to make the provisions he or she did in the will.

Example: Michael constantly visits his uncle Bill, an 88 year old retired business tycoon, in the nursing home. During his visits, Michael continuously urges Bill to leave his vast business interests to him – to the detriment of Bill's own children who don't visit as often as they should. Michael, knowing that Bill is lonely and depressed, threatens to stop visiting him as he is clearly ungrateful for Michael's kindness and attention. Michael finally arrives at the nursing home with his lawyer, who has never met Bill before. Michael remains present while Bill instructs the lawyer to write a new will for him in which he purports to leave all his business interests to Michael.

Ideally, an ethical lawyer should never agree to make a will or codicil in such circumstances, but in reality, it does happen. Therefore it's always wise to get independent legal advice when you make a will or codicil.

Wills Made in Other States

Generally speaking, wills made in one state are effective in all other states in the United States. However, when it comes to probate, in addition to filing the will for probate in the state in which the testator resided, the will may also need to be filed for probate in each state in which the testator held assets. This is particularly true in cases where the testator held valuable real estate in states outside his or her state of residence. Fortunately, if the assets located in a particular state are minimal in value, there may be a simplified means of 'probating' those assets without conducting a full scale probate. Availing of these simplified procedures will save your estate considerable money and avoid delays in the long run.

If you require specific information regarding the probate of assets in other states, we recommend that you seek legal advice from a qualified and experienced lawyer.

GIFTS AND BENEFICIARIES

Gifts to Spouses

Before making a gift to your spouse, or indeed to any one, it is important to understand the rights which surviving spouses have over their deceased spouse's estate; as well as the basic differences in distribution of property in both common law and community property states. We'll look at these matters below.

Community Property States

Property owned by couples in community property states is divided loosely into two categories - separate property and community property.

A spouse's separate property is all property acquired by that spouse before or after he or she got married (including after a legal separation) plus all property received as a gift or an inheritance and maintained separately (i.e. not jointly with his or her spouse) during that marriage. Community property, on the other hand, is all other property earned or acquired by either spouse during the marriage.

Important Note

At the date of writing there are nine community property states namely Arizona, California, Idaho, Louisiana, Nevada, New Mexico, Texas, Washington and Wisconsin. In Alaska couples can opt to have their property treated as community property under the terms of a written property agreement. The property distribution rules in these states may also apply to registered domestic partners.

Separate property can also be deemed community property where it is formerly transferred by one spouse to the joint names of both spouses. Similarly, where property is gifted to one spouse and subsequently commingled with community property, the property can become community property.

Each of Alaska, Arizona, California, Nevada, Texas and Wisconsin allow a surviving spouse or domestic partner to automatically inherit community property when the other spouse or partner dies provided that property's title document makes it clear that the property is owned as community property with a right of survivorship in favor of the surviving spouse.

Normally, classifying property as community or separate property is relatively straightforward. However there are a number of instances in which the classification is not clear. These include the ownership of businesses, companies, pensions, the proceeds of certain lawsuits, and incomes received from separate property. In cases such as these, you should consult a local attorney to determine how your state treats these items.

The majority of community property states do not grant a surviving spouse a legal right to inherit from the deceased spouse's estate. Rather, what they do is try to divide the marital assets (or registered partnership assets) during the lifetime of the spouses (or partners) by classifying certain assets as community property. Each spouse (or partner) in turn is deemed to own 50% of the community property.

However, in each of Alaska, California, Idaho, Washington and Wisconsin a surviving spouse or domestic partner may elect to receive a specific portion of the deceased spouse's community or separate property in limited circumstances. For more information on such entitlements, we recommend that you consult a lawyer.

 Warning

If you are in a registered domestic partnership and considering a move to another state, you should pay close attention to the laws of the state into which you are proposing to move as the 'new state' may not recognize the property rights which you had in your 'old state'. If you are in any doubt as to how the law will affect you, you should consult a practicing lawyer in your area.

Common Law States

In common law states, each spouse owns all property acquired using their own income and all property legally registered solely in their name. Any property, such as your marital home for example, registered in the names of both spouses is deemed to be owned jointly. If you reside in a common law state, your spouse has a legal right to a fraction of your estate upon your passing. Depending on which state you reside in, this legal right will usually amount to between one-third and one-half of your estate. The precise amount to which your spouse is entitled will also depend on whether you have any children and whether your spouse has been provided for outside the terms of your will or living trust.

The legal right of your spouse will take priority over any devises or legacies made in your will or your living trust, and will rank in priority after creditors of your estate. Your spouse will be entitled to either exercise his or her legal right to receive the specified fraction of your estate which he or she is entitled to or waive that right in favor of whatever has been left to him or her under the terms of your will and/or living trust.

The right of your spouse to take a defined percentage of your estate does not arise by the operation of law; rather it must be proactively elected. This means that your spouse must 'speak up' and state that he or she wishes to exercise this right rather than accept what has been left to them under the terms of your will or living trust. Of course, any such election should be in writing and signed by your spouse. If your spouse fails to elect to take his or her legal share within the time frames set out under law, then he or she will be obliged to accept the gifts you have left to him or her under your will and/or living trust. Separately, your spouse can also waive his or her rights to this entitlement if he or she wishes.

Matters in relation to elections of a legal right can become more complex when a couple moves from a common law state to a community property state. In California, Idaho, Washington and Wisconsin, property acquired prior to a move will be treated as if it had been acquired in the state to which you have moved. In other community property states, the property will be treated in accordance with the laws of the state in which it was acquired. As you no doubt have gathered, this can result in marital property being subjected to both common law and community property rules. In such cases, it is important that care is taken to determine which laws affect what types of property before you commence making your will or transferring property to your living trust.

By contrast, couples that move from a community property state to a common law state come up against the opposite problem. In such cases, each spouse or partner retains a 50% interest in the community property acquired while the couple was resident in the community property state.

Important Note

If you have any concerns relating to the entitlements of your spouse or dependents to a share in your estate, we recommend that you speak to a lawyer.

Disinheritance

While the laws vary slightly from state to state, it's generally only a spouse or registered partner that has any real entitlement to inherit from a deceased person's estate after they die. Surprisingly for some, children do not automatically have a right to inherit from their parents.

For one reason or another, many people consider disinheriting family members – often because of some underlying dispute. It's therefore important to look at how the laws work in this area so that you can, if you so wish, disinherit family members to the fullest extent permitted by law. We'll do just that in the ensuing pages.

Disinheriting a Spouse

As discussed above, the laws of most states allow a surviving spouse the choice of choosing between what he or she has been left under the terms of his or her deceased spouse's will or receiving a specific share of the deceased spouse's estate as defined by statute. This share is known as the minimum or "elective" share. While the amount of this share tends to vary from state to state, the general rule is that if a deceased spouse had no children the surviving would be entitled to half of the deceased spouse's net estate. On the other hand, where the deceased spouse had children, the surviving spouse would have an entitlement to claim one third of the deceased spouse's net estate. Some states also impose financial thresholds. For example, under New York law, a surviving spouse is entitled to $50,000 or one third of the deceased spouse's net estate, whichever is the greater.

Did You Know?

Divorce terminates the right of election by the surviving spouse.

Where the deceased spouse leaves more than the elective share of the net estate to the surviving spouse, he or she will generally not exercise the right of election unless he or she believed that it would be more advantageous to allow a greater part of the deceased spouse's estate to pass to the other beneficiaries named in the will, for tax reasons or otherwise. Of course, the surviving spouse's right of election is really only valuable where the deceased spouse left less than the elective share to the surviving spouse. Consider, for example, the situation where a husband dies leaving everything to his children and nothing his spouse. In such a case, the surviving spouse would under New York law, for example, have the right to receive the elective share (i.e., the greater of $50,000 or one-third of the estate) notwithstanding the terms of the deceased spouse's will or living trust. The consequence of this is that the amount of the deceased spouse's estate passing to the children would be reduced. It may even be the case that certain beneficiaries no longer receive a gift from the deceased spouse!

If a surviving spouse elects to take his or her legal share rather than take what was left to him or her under the terms of the deceased spouse's will, then he or she generally forfeits the right to receive anything under the will. However, in many cases where an election is made, the surviving spouse will often be allowed take some or all of the items (depending on what was gifted to the surviving spouse) left to him or her under the will, particularly in circumstances where the amount left under the will is in fact less than the spouse's elective share. The balance of any amount owing to the surviving spouse is often then made up in cash. Alternatively, he or she can take assets from the residuary estate and so on until the legal share is satisfied. On the other hand, if the spouse elects to take his or her inheritance under the deceased spouse's will he or she will generally be entitled to receive those assets from the estate.

Whichever choice a surviving spouse makes, it's important to remember that they will (unless the terms of the will provides otherwise) still be entitled to avail of their other legal rights which, depending on the state law, include the right to buy certain estate assets, to remain in the principal residence for a specific period of time (usually a year), to claim and receive an allowance for their support, to receive automobiles and watercraft owned by the deceased, and to avail of such other rights as a surviving spouse would ordinarily be entitled to under law.

While in most cases, the election of the surviving spouse will not affect certain non-probate property, such as jointly owned property and property with rights of survivorship attached, pay-on-death accounts and transfer-on-death securities, it may well have an effect on other types of non-probate property such as property held in a trust. That said, in states which have adopted the Uniform Probate Code, certain assets that have passed to the surviving spouse either during the life of the deceased spouse or on the death of the deceased spouse (thorough joint tenancy or on survivorship) are deemed part of the surviving spouse's elective share. You will need to check the laws of your state of residence to determine what property is included in the surviving spouse's right to elect.

Did You Know?

The Uniform Probate Code (the "Code") is a statute that unifies the laws governing the transfer of a person's estate. It deals with matters such as probate, transfers on intestacy, transfer of assets outside of probate, legal entitlements of spouses and trust administration. The Code was originally approved by the National Conference of Commissioners on Uniform State Laws and the House of Delegates of the American Bar Association in 1969. Its purpose was to modernize probate law and administration and to encourage uniformity in all fifty states.

As you will have gathered from the foregoing, in most states, a person cannot simply disinherit their spouse.

Types of Gifts

A gift can generally be defined as a voluntary transfer of property from one person to another made gratuitously, without any consideration or compensation. Under your will, you can leave gifts of either financial or personal value to your family and friends. These gifts can come in the form of gifts of a specific item, gifts of cash or gifts of the residuary of your estate. Each of these forms of gift is explained below.

Specific Item Gifts

A specific item gift (also known as a legacy or bequest) is a gift of a specific item to a named beneficiary. Gifts of this type typically include items such as, for example, a car, a piece of jewelry, stocks, bonds, land, houses and so on. When you are inserting details of a specific item gift in your will, it is important to ensure that you clearly identify and describe the item that you wish to gift. So, for example, where you are gifting a car, you should describe the make, model and color of the car rather than simply referring to "my car". This reduces the risk of confusion over what you intended in your will – especially if you have more than one car at the time of your death! When writing a provision for a gift, a good question to ask yourself is whether a stranger reading your will would easily understand exactly what you wanted to gift. If not, you need to re-write that clause!

Cash Gifts

A cash gift (also known as monetary or pecuniary legacy) is a gift of a specific amount of money to a named beneficiary. Just as with specific items gifts, when making a cash gift you need to clearly specify the amount that you are gifting (including the currency) and the person to whom you wish to make the gift to. In addition, when making a cash gift, it is important that you consider the financial implications on the overall estate. Remember, you may need to ensure that sufficient funds are readily available to meet the needs of your dependents or to discharge any taxes or expenses (including funeral expenses) which might be payable following your death. So be careful not to exhaust your cash too quickly – otherwise other assets may need to be sold to raise funds to discharge these obligations.

Gift of the Residuary Estate

This is simply a gift of the residue or remainder of an estate to one or more named beneficiaries. The residue of an estate (or residuary estate, as it's often called) is the remainder of a deceased person's estate after the payment of all debts, funeral and testamentary expenses and after all specific item and cash gifts have been made. The residuary also includes property that is the subject of a failed gift. A gift fails in circumstances where the beneficiary has died before becoming entitled to the gift or refuses to accept the gift. The person entitled to receive a gift of the residuary estate under a will is called the residuary beneficiary or, if there is more than one beneficiary, the residuary beneficiaries.

What Assets Can I Gift Under My Will?

When it comes to making your will, it's important to understand that only assets which form part of your estate can be gifted in your will. In general terms, your estate comprises of all of the assets that you own outright such as your real estate, property, cash, investments, insurance policies, valuables, cars, jewelry and so on.

There is however a number of assets which fall outside of your estate. Knowing what these assets are is important for two very specific reasons. Firstly, and most obviously, by knowing what assets you cannot gift under your will, you can easily identify those assets which you can gift. Secondly, by knowing the types of asset which fall outside of your estate, you can plan your estate in a manner that allows for some of your assets to pass to your proposed beneficiaries without having them tied up in the probate process. This is because only those assets which pass under your will need to go through probate. This is important because you can construct your estate in a way that allows your estate to pass to your beneficiaries quite quickly and in a manner which reduces probate fees!

The most common forms of assets which don't pass under your estate and don't go through probate include the following:-

(i)   joint bank accounts;
(ii) life insurance policies;
(iii) pensions;
(iv) jointly owned property; and
(v)   property in a revocable living trust.

Joint Bank Accounts

An easy way to avoid probate is by having joint bank accounts. Where an account is held in the name of two or more persons and is designated with the right of survivorship, then when one of the account holders die, the surviving account holders will automatically acquire the deceased account holder's interest in the account. Whoever is the last surviving joint owner will ultimately own the proceeds of the account outright.

Where a transfer occurs on survivorship, there is no need for probate. The surviving account holder(s) will simply need to provide a copy of the deceased account holder's death certificate to the bank and the bank can then remove that person's name from the account.

 Important Note

You can convert assets that you own solely into jointly owned assets and thereby avoid probate of those assets.

Life Insurance Policies

A life policy is another example of a simple means by which you can avoid probate. Where you designate a named beneficiary under your life insurance policy, the proceeds of the policy which are payable on your death will pass directly to the named beneficiary without the need to go through probate. However, if your estate is named as the main beneficiary (which is unusual) or if no beneficiaries have been named or if the named beneficiaries have died, the proceeds will need to pass to your estate and go through probate.

Pensions

Similar to the position with insurance policies, it's possible to designate beneficiaries for a number of other assets including pensions. In the same way as with insurance, when you die, the assets will be passed to the named beneficiaries without the need for probate.

Jointly Owned Property

Whether or not the property that you own at the time of your death will need to be probated depends on how the title to that property is held. Typically, property can be held in two different ways namely (i) joint tenancy (with the right of survivorship) or (ii) a tenancy in common.

Joint tenancy: We've already touched on the concept of joint tenancy in relation to bank accounts above. The same principle applies to real estate. Where a property is held under a joint tenancy, each of the property owners has an undivided percentage interest in the entire property. To illustrate this, an example is often useful. So let's, for example, take a case where four people own a property equally under a joint tenancy arrangement. Each of the four owners has an entitlement to a 25% interest in the entire or whole of the property. However, they are generally not free to sell that interest or transfer that interest on death.

Where one of the joint tenants dies, their share passes to the remaining joint tenants. Taking our example again, where one of the four property owners die, their share passes to each of the other three survivors automatically and each of the survivors then becomes entitled to an approximate 33.33% (or 1/3) interest in the property.

The key point to take from the above is that the share passes from the deceased joint owner to the remaining joint owners without the need for probate. It follows that probate can either be reduced or even eliminated by converting solely owned assets into jointly owned assets – held under a joint tenancy. This type of ownership permits the jointly owned assets to simply pass directly to the surviving joint owners on the death of one of the owners – no need for probate.

Tenancy in common: A tenancy in common is one of the most common forms of property ownership in the United States. A tenancy in common is created where two or more people purchase a property together as 'tenants in common'. As tenants in common, each of the parties own a separate and distinguishable part of the property. To take the example of our four property owners above, if the arrangement was a tenancy in common, each of them would own 25% of the property in their own right and would be free to sell that 25% to any person at any time and/or to <u>dispose of their interest under their will</u>. The right of survivorship does not apply here. As this type of interest in property can transfer under a will, it will need to go through probate.

Property in a Revocable Living Trust

An additional way to avoid probate is to establish and fund a revocable living trust. This type of trust is established under a written trust agreement. In essence, under the terms of the trust agreement, the creator of the trust (known as a grantor) will transfer ownership of certain of his assets into the trust. The trustee of the trust (which is also actually the grantor) will hold and manage the assets on behalf of the trust. The trustee can manage, invest, and spend the trust property as he or she sees fit for the benefit of the grantor and for the benefit of the ultimate beneficiaries of the trust.

Because the grantor will not own any of the trust property in his or her individual name after the trust assets have been transferred into the name of the trust, the assets won't need to be probated. When the grantor dies, the person nominated as the 'successor trustee' under the terms of the trust agreement will step into the grantor's shoes and will distribute the proceeds of the trust (i.e. the trust assets) to the named beneficiaries in accordance with the terms of the trust agreement.

Important Note

If you require further information on assets that do not go through probate, speak to a lawyer or view Enodare's book on estate planning called "Estate Planning Essentials".

Types of Beneficiaries

A beneficiary is a person, organization or other entity that will inherit part of your assets or estate under your will. There are three main types of beneficiaries under a will. These include a specific gift beneficiary, an alternate beneficiary and a residuary beneficiary.

Specific Gift Beneficiary

A specific gift beneficiary is a person or organization named in your will to receive a cash gift or a specific item gift as defined above. Specific gifts are generally the first gifts distributed under a will. Any assets that are not specifically distributed under your will shall form part of the residuary estate (assuming that you have a catch all residuary clause – see below) and will usually be given (unless there are taxes or other expenses to be discharged) to the person or persons named as residuary beneficiary or beneficiaries, as the case may be.

Alternate Beneficiary

When naming beneficiaries to receive gifts under your will, it can be prudent (but is not obligatory) to prepare for the possibility that one or more of these beneficiaries will be unable (whether due to death or otherwise) or unwilling (for whatever reason) to accept the gifts made to them. To this end, it can be helpful to nominate alternate beneficiaries to receive the gift in the event that the primary beneficiary is unable or unwilling to accept it. An alternate beneficiary is a person who becomes legally entitled to inherit a gift if the first named beneficiary is unable or unwilling to accept the gift. If no alternate beneficiary is named for the gift, the gift will form part of the residuary estate and go to the residuary beneficiary.

You are entirely free to name more than one person as an alternate beneficiary. For example, you can appoint a second alternate beneficiary to receive a gift where the first alternate beneficiary is unable or unwilling to accept it. However, when doing this it is important that you fully consider the order in which the alternate beneficiaries become entitled to share the property and ensure that this order is correct.

Residuary Beneficiary

A residuary beneficiary is the person(s) or organization(s) named to receive the residue of your estate; they get what's left when all of the specific item gifts and cash gifts have been made and all debts and taxes have been paid.

Who May Not Be a Beneficiary?

While you are generally free to make gifts to anyone you choose, the law does place some restrictions on the people who can receive gifts from you under your will. In particular, the following persons or organizations will be precluded from receiving gifts from you under your will:

- a lawyer who is involved in drafting your will or in providing advice to you in connection with your will;

- a person who has witnessed the signing of your will;

- a person who unlawfully caused your death; and

- a company or unincorporated association that is not permitted to hold property under the terms of its constitutional documents.

Gifts to Charities

When it comes to making a will, many of us want to make a gift to our favorite charity. Doing this is relatively straightforward. All you need to do is identify the gift you wish to make and the charity that will receive the gift. You can gift money, specific items or nominate the charity as a beneficiary of the residuary of your estate – the choice is yours! However, if you choose to make a gift to a charity it's important to ensure that you provide clear details of the charity to be benefited. In this respect, it's useful to identity the charity by reference to its correct legal name (as it may differ from the 'trading name' commonly used by the charity) as well as its charity registration number. You can usually get these details from the charity's website.

Imposing Conditions on the Receipt of Gifts

In making a gift under your will, you may wish to provide that the beneficiary will only be entitled to receive that gift if certain conditions are satisfied. While this is perfectly acceptable, you do need to take extreme care when adding conditions. In fact, it's best to consult a lawyer when you are doing so.

There are two basic types of conditions that can be imposed on a beneficiary - conditions precedent and conditions subsequent.

A condition precedent is a requirement that must be met before the beneficiary is entitled to receive a gift. For example, you may specify that "*I give the sum of $5,000 to my nephew Michael Smith if he has obtained a college degree in engineering before 31 December 2020. If my nephew Michael Smith has not obtained the college degree as aforesaid, then I give the sum of $5,000 to my niece Emma Smith instead*". The imposition of such a condition does not pose too many difficulties for the executor or trustee as it will be easy to determine whether the beneficiary has met the requirement or not…. of course they may have to wait a while to find out. If the beneficiary fails to meet the requirements, then the proceeds being held by the executor or trustee to make this gift will be given to the alternate beneficiary or, where none is named, to the persons entitled to the residuary interest in the estate (i.e. the residuary beneficiaries).

A condition subsequent, on the other hand, is a requirement that must be met after the beneficiary receives the gift. These types of conditions cause a lot more problems than conditions precedent because often the gift is received on the condition that the beneficiary fulfils an obligation or a specific event occurs. Problems arise where the obligation is not fulfilled or the event never occurs.

If we took our example above and modified the condition such that it became a condition subsequent, it would read something like this "*I give the sum of $5,000 to my nephew Michael Smith on the condition that he uses this money to obtain a college degree in engineering before 31 December 2020. If my nephew Michael Smith has not obtained the college* *degree as aforesaid, then I give the sum of $5,000 to my niece Emma Smith instead*". In this instance, Michael has received the gift before he has satisfied the condition. This of course can be problematic. What happens if Michael fails to satisfy the condition within the required time frame? Well, Emma will need to try and recover the $5,000 from Michael. This may be easier said than done of course.

While conditions being placed on the receipt of a gift are generally valid, there are some conditions that courts will refuse to enforce. Typically, these are conditions that are void for uncertainty (i.e. they are unclear) or void on the grounds of public policy. Conditions void on the grounds of public policy would, for example, include requirements that the beneficiary marry or refrain from marrying someone, divorce or refrain from divorcing someone, change religion or even murder someone. Conditions void for uncertainty are void simply because they are unclear and their performance cannot therefore be strictly observed.

 Warning

We do not recommend that you include conditional gifts in your will without first speaking to a lawyer.

Releasing Someone from a Debt

Under your will you may release or "forgive" a debt owed to you by another person, incorporated body, or un-incorporated association. This will legally release that person or entity from the debt on your death. If you do not forgive the debt, your executor will be entitled to institute legal proceedings on behalf of your estate in order to recover the monies from the debtor in question.

Failed Gifts

If you decide to gift a specific item to a beneficiary in your will and you subsequently dispose of that item before your death then, upon your death, the gift will fail because it cannot be completed. Where the gift fails, the intended beneficiary will not be entitled to receive a substitute gift under your will unless you have expressly provided for this in your will.

Additionally, if you gift a specific item or a particular amount of money to a named person and that person predeceases you then, unless an alternate beneficiary is entitled to receive that gift under the terms of your will, the gift fails and reverts to form part of your residuary estate. An exception to this general principal arises under the 'per stirpes' rule which provides that where a person makes a gift to their child and that child predeceases the parent, the gift will pass to the deceased child's estate. Depending on whether the child made a will or died intestate, the gift will be distributed to the deceased's child's beneficiaries/heirs.

Matters Affecting the Distribution of Your Assets

Before you make any decisions on how you wish to distribute your assets, it's useful to be aware of a number of specific events that can have an impact on how your assets are ultimately distributed. These events include the following: -

- simultaneous death;

- abatement of assets; and

- disclaimed inheritances.

We'll consider each of these further below.

Simultaneous Death

It is common in wills to insert what is known as a 'common disaster' or 'simultaneous death' provision. These types of provisions usually provide that in order for your beneficiary to receive a gift under your will, they must survive you for a period of say 30 to 60 days before they can inherit. This is aimed at the situation where, for example, you might die in an accident in which one or more of your named beneficiaries (particularly your spouse) are also fatally injured. If that beneficiary survives you, and there is no required survival period, he or she would be entitled to receive the gift immediately on your death. If that beneficiary then dies shortly after you, the beneficiary's heirs would in turn be entitled to receive the gift on probate of the first deceased beneficiary's estate. The provision is therefore designed to avoid multiple probates/administrations and taxes on the same assets where one or more of your beneficiaries die of injuries a few hours (or days) after you.

This common disaster provision is most commonly used between spouses and typically provides for the transfer of the estate to the surviving spouse but only if he or she survives the deceased spouse for a specified period of time following the death of the 'deceased spouse'. If the 'surviving spouse' does not survive the 'deceased spouse' for the requisite time frame, the gift will pass to any alternate beneficiary named under the will to receive that gift or, where none is named, to the residuary beneficiaries.

Abatement of Assets

When the residuary of an estate is insufficient to pay the debts and taxes owing by an estate, it will become necessary to apply other assets of the estate to meet these payments. The process by which these assets are applied to pay the debts of the estate is known as abatement. When assets are abated, they are sold (if not already in cash form) to raise cash to discharge the debts of the estate. Generally, the first assets of an estate which are abated are legacies (i.e. the cash gifts). For example, if the estate has $50,000 in the bank account to cover cash gifts to the deceased's friends, and debts are still owing by the estate after the residuary estate has been dissipated, this money may be used to discharge these debts. Any of the $50,000 remaining after payment of the debts will be distributed pro rata to the aforementioned beneficiaries. However, if the funds are insufficient to pay off all of the debts, then the executor can begin to sell the items left as specific item gifts (i.e. antiques, jeweler, property, etc) in order to raise the required funds.

As you will have gathered, the net result following the abatement process is that people who have been left gifts under your will may not receive anything if the estate has high levels of debt. As such, in making your will, you need to carefully consider the debt levels of your estate and even consider designating in your will the assets that you would like sold to meet those debts if there are insufficient reserves in the residuary estate to meet the payments.

Disclaimed Inheritances

A beneficiary can renounce or disclaim their entitlement to receive a gift under a will. This may be done for several reasons - because it's unwanted, carries heavy liabilities (property maintenance, for example), tax reasons, or because the intended beneficiary simply wants to pass the gift to another beneficiary. If an alternate beneficiary has been named in your will to receive that gift, he or she will then become entitled to it. If no alternate beneficiary is named, the gift will be passed to the beneficiary or beneficiaries entitled to the residue of the estate.

What if You Own Property Outside The United States?

As more and more people now own foreign properties it has become increasingly important to take account of these foreign assets in the preparation of wills. Of more importance, however, is the necessity to ensure that you do not inadvertently revoke an existing will when making a local or foreign will. This brief section explains how this could happen.

Generally, your foreign property is subject to the succession laws of the country in which the property is located. As such, it becomes necessary to execute a will dealing with your property in that country in order to record your wishes in relation to the foreign property. To prevent any new U.S. will revoking a foreign will relating only to property located in a foreign country, it is necessary to insert a clause in your U.S. will to the effect that it does not relate to any property held outside of the United States. A similar clause should be inserted into any foreign wills that you make so that they don't revoke any wills you have made in the United States.

As there are various estate taxation systems in existence in other countries, it is highly advisable to seek the advice of a national lawyer in the country in which your foreign assets are held.

 Did You Know?

If you happen to own any assets (including real estate, insurance or even stocks or shares) that are situated outside the United States and would like to make a will in respect of those assets please feel free to visit our website, www.enodare.com or any of our sister websites: www.enodare.ca; www.enodare.co.uk; or www.enodare.ie for further assistance.

CHILDREN, GUARDIANS AND PROPERTY MANAGEMENT

What Is a Guardian?

A guardian is the person responsible for a child's (or other dependent or incapacitated person's) physical care, education, health and welfare; as well as for making decisions about the child's faith-related matters.

In the normal scheme of things, if you are married and have a child you and your spouse are the primary legal guardians of your minor children, including any children that you may have adopted together. If you pass away, then your surviving spouse becomes the sole guardian of these children. However, should your surviving spouse also pass away, and neither of you have made any provisions for the appointment of a guardian, then the children could become the responsibility of the courts who will typically appoint a family relative to care for your children where possible. Where this happens, there is a real risk that your children could end up being cared for by people that you would never have wished to raise them.

If you have children, it is therefore vital to plan ahead and ensure that they will be properly cared for in the event that neither you nor your spouse are around to do so. In this respect, you should give careful thought and consideration to naming a guardian and an alternate guardian in your will to take care of your children following your passing.

Sole and Joint Guardians

You have the option of appointing one or more guardians to care for your children. If you appoint one guardian, he or she will be known as a "sole guardian" and will be solely responsible for the welfare of your children and for making all decisions (including financial decisions) on their behalf. Alternatively, you can also nominate two or more people to serve as joint-guardians to the children. However, with joint guardians, each of them must reach agreement in relation to decisions regarding the children in their care. It is for this reason that joint-guardians are usually only nominated where they are married to each other or live together, as well as where they each have an important relationship to the children (uncles or aunts, for example).

If you are considering appointing a married couple as joint-guardians of your children, be sure to carefully consider the status of the couple's relationship and whether you would want both spouses to serve as guardians if they were ever separated or divorced. In such instances, it may be preferable to simply appoint one spouse as guardian at the very outset. The choice, however, is yours.

Alternate Guardians

When appointing a guardian, it is generally recommended that you also appoint an alternate guardian (or several alternates, hierarchically) who will serve if, for any reason, your first named guardian (known as your 'primary guardian') is unable or unwilling to serve when the time comes. If your first choice guardian cannot serve and you fail to name an alternate guardian in your will, it will then fall to the court to step in and determine who will act as guardian to your children. As alluded to above, the court's appointee may not be someone that you would have approved of had you the opportunity to do so!

Who Can Be a Guardian?

Well, the short answer is that anyone can be a guardian provided that they are agreeable to acting as a guardian to your children and are themselves an adult.

What to Consider When Choosing a Guardian for Your Children

As you will be leaving the responsibility of caring for your children to another person, the decision as to whom you should appoint as a guardian to your children is an extremely important one; and one that should not be made lightly. You will need to take many factors into consideration. Ultimately, however, you should choose the person you believe will offer the best care and support to your children. Often this will be a close relative or family friend. However, before actually appointing them as guardian under your will, it is very important that you check with your proposed nominee to ensure that he or she is willing to accept such a responsible and onerous role. There is no point in nominating someone if you think they will refuse to accept the role when the time comes.

Important Note!

Discuss your choice with the people you have selected as guardians and make sure they are willing to accept the responsibility should it become necessary.

There are many things that you will need to take into account when considering whether a person would be a good guardian to your children. In particular, you should ask yourself the following questions regarding the proposed nominee:

- is the person you are considering willing to accept the long-term responsibility of being a guardian to your children?

- is this person responsible and up to the task of raising your children?

- is the person old enough (at least over 18 years) to be a guardian?

- where does this person reside?

- would your children be uprooted and moved away from their friends and family members if they went to live with this guardian? Would that be in their best interests?

- if you have more than one child, do you want your children to remain together? If you do then be sure to name the same guardian for all of your children.

- what is this person's home situation? For example, does he or she have a house or a one-bed apartment? Is the potential guardian in a stable relationship?

- will the potential guardian be able to provide your children with a stable positive environment and home life?

- will your children still have easy access to their other relatives – such as grandparents?

- what are the person's religious and moral beliefs?

- does the person have any medical conditions or other issues that would prevent them from being a suitable guardian?

- if you cannot make sufficient financial provision for your children's long-term care, will this person be able to afford to care for your children?

These are all very important and relative questions, but only the tip of the iceberg. There will no doubt be many other things that will influence your decision. So take your time to think things through thoroughly.

Once you have selected someone to act as a guardian to your children, it is important to discuss the potential appointment with him or her (or them) in detail. While most people are flattered, you will find that some are unable or unwilling to accept the responsibility. Be wary also of people agreeing to accept the role insincerely in the expectation that they will never be called upon to act. This is another very good reason to appoint an alternate guardian - just in case the primary guardian is unable or unwilling to assume the role when the time comes.

Management of Children's Property

While the appointment of a guardian to care for and to raise your child is important, it is equally important to consider who will manage the money and property your child inherits from you; and indeed from anyone else. This is because children who have not yet reached the age of majority lack sufficient legal capacity to receive and manage inherited property. While this lack of capacity is often not an issue for most minors, it is problematic where they inherit significant or valuable assets. In such cases, it will be necessary to appoint an adult called a 'custodian', 'trustee' or 'property guardian' to receive and manage the property on behalf of the minor.

If you don't make arrangements to provide for the future management of your children's property, the court will do it for you by appointing a 'property guardian' of its choosing to manage the inheritances. Similar to the situation with normal guardians, a court will often appoint the surviving parent but this is not always the case. A third party or court appointed guardian can be appointed to deal with the property and, in such cases, that property guardian will have complete control over your children's inheritance. As such, it is important that you deal with this appointment in your will or in another legal agreement.

Fortunately, it is relatively easy and straightforward to avoid the uncertainties and hassles of a court-appointed guardianship. You can choose someone now to manage any property that your minor or young adult children may someday inherit from you. While there are many ways that you can structure this arrangement, four of the simplest and most commonly used methods are listed below.

Appointment of a Property Guardian

A property guardian is a person you appoint to be responsible for managing the property you leave to your children plus any other property that your children might receive. A property guardian is bound to manage the property in your children's best interests, using it to pay for normal living expenses, as well as health and educational needs.

If you name a property guardian for your children in your will, when the time comes, the court will (in the absence of strong reasons to do otherwise) formally appoint your selected person as property guardian to your children.

While a property guardian is appointed under the terms of your will, the scope of his or her management authority extends beyond the management of property left to your children under your will. In fact, it extends to include any property later received by your children where there are no pre-existing arrangements for management of that property (such as under a trust). As such, should your children receive an inheritance from a long lost relative, their property guardian is authorized to manage that property in the absence of your relative having provided for a specific means of management.

Remember, a property guardian is different to a personal guardian; the latter guardian is responsible for the care, health, welfare and education of the child. A property guardian is only responsible for managing the child's property – although he or she can apply the managed property for the benefit of the child's care, health, welfare or education. Do not make the mistake of appointing only a property guardian and thinking that he or she will also be responsible for the day-to-day care of the child!

Uniform Transfer to Minors' Act

As often mentioned, minors in most states do not have the legal capacity to enter into certain legal contracts, and are therefore not in position where they can own and manage assets such as stocks, bonds, funds, life insurance receipts and other annuities. It is therefore important to recognize that you cannot simply transfer any of these types of items directly to your minor children; or indeed to any other minor.

One of the most common methods used to get around this problem comes in the form of a custodianship created under either the Uniform Gift to Minors Act ("UGMA") or the Uniform Transfer to Minors Act ("UTMA"). Rather than transferring assets directly to your children on your death, you transfer your assets to a custodian who will hold those assets on trust for your children until they reach a pre-determined age. Once your children reach this age, the custodian will transfer the property that he or she is holding on their behalf to them. In the interim period, the custodian will be obliged to manage the property on your children's behalf in accordance with the provisions set out in the UGMA/UTMA.

The UGMA, which was enacted before the UTMA, created a very simple way for assets to be transferred to children under a trust arrangement without the need for lawyers and without the associated legal costs. To set up a custodianship under the UGMA, all a person needed to do was identify the property which he or she wished to transfer to a child (it can be any child named under a will – not just the child of the testator) and to name a custodian to manage that property in the event that the child in question had not reached a designated age (usually between 18 to 25 years depending on state law) at the time they became entitled to receive the gift.

A typical clause of this type would be as follows:-

> *"I give $25,000 to James Jones, as custodian for Sarah Parker under the California Uniform Transfers to Minors Act, to hold until Sarah Parker reaches the age of 21 years."*

While the UTMA is similar in its approach to the UGMA, it is widely considered to be more flexible than the UGMA, which was repealed to a large degree by the UTMA. While the UTMA affords minors much of the same benefits as the previous act, it also allows minors to own other types of property (apart from cash) such as real estate, patents and royalties and more importantly, for the transfers to occur through inheritance and not simply by means of a gift.

The UTMA has been adopted in all states except for Vermont and South Carolina.

The age at which the custodianship terminates is the age at which a 'minor' becomes legally entitled to call for the assets held by a custodian to be transferred to him or her, and to have the custodial trust terminated. The table below shows the ages of termination of custodianships in the various states which have adopted the UTMA. As you will see, the ages vary from 18 to 25 years of age. You will also see that in some states the age is specified, while in other states a range of ages is provided from which the will maker can chose a particular age.

You should be aware that the age of termination of a custodianship is not necessarily the same as the age of majority in a particular state.

State	UGMA	UTMA	UGMA Repeal *
Alabama	19	21	October 1, 1986
Alaska	18	18-25	January 1, 1991
Arizona	18	21	September 30, 1988
Arkansas	21	18-21	March 21, 1985
California	18	18-25	January 1, 1985
Colorado	21	21	July 1, 1984
Connecticut	21	21	October 1, 1995
Delaware	18	21	June 26, 1996
District of Columbia	18	18-21	March 12, 1986
Florida	18	21	October 1, 1985
Georgia	21	21	July 1, 1990
Guam	21	N/A	N/A
Hawaii	18	21	July 1, 1985
Idaho	18	21	July 1, 1984
Illinois	21	21	July 1, 1986
Indiana	18	21	July 1, 1989
Iowa	21	21	July 1, 1986
Kansas	18	21	July 1, 1985
Kentucky	21	18	July 15, 1986
Louisiana	18	18	January 1, 1988
Maine	21	18-21	August 4, 1988
Maryland	18	21	July 1, 1989
Massachusetts	18	21	January 30, 1987
Michigan	18	18-21	December 29, 1999
Minnesota	18	21	January 1, 1986

State	UGMA	UTMA	UGMA Repeal *
Mississippi	21	21	January 1, 1995
Missouri	21	21	September 28, 1985
Montana	18	21	October 1, 1985
Nebraska	19	21	July 15, 1992
Nevada	18	18-25	July 1, 1985
New Hampshire	21	21	July 30, 1985
New Jersey	21	18-21	July 1, 1987
New Mexico	21	21	July 1, 1989
New York	18	21	July 10, 1996
North Carolina	18	18-21	October 1, 1987
North Dakota	18	21	July 1, 1985
Ohio	18	18-21	May 7, 1986
Oklahoma	21	18-21	November 1, 1986
Oregon	21	21-25	January 1, 1986
Pennsylvania	21	21-25	December 16, 1992
Rhode Island	21	21	July 23, 1998
South Carolina	18	N/A	N/A
South Dakota	18	18	July 1, 1986
Tennessee	18	21-25	October 1, 1992
Texas	18	21	September 1, 1995
Utah	21	21	July 1, 1990
Vermont	18	N/A	N/A
Virgin Islands	21	N/A	N/A
Virginia	18	18-21	July 1, 1988
Washington	21	21	July 1, 1991
West Virginia	18	21	July 1, 1986
Wisconsin	18	21	April 8, 1988
Wyoming	18	21	May 22, 1987

Individual Child Trusts

A child's trust is valid in all U.S. states and can be created under the terms of a will (these trusts are often called testamentary trust).

A trust is a fiduciary arrangement whereby a person is appointed to become the legal owner of trust property, which they will hold for the benefit of another person. A child trust is a trust created for the benefit of a child. You can create a separate child trust for each of your children (if you wish) and for any other minor who stands to inherit under the terms of your will.

In your will you can name a trustee (usually a trusted relative or friend) who will manage the inheritance that a child will receive (as a beneficiary of that trust) until that child reaches an age specified by you. If the child in question has reached that age at the time of your death, and is past the age of majority for their state, the trust never actually comes into existence and the property is instead transferred directly to them upon your death.

However, where your child is under the age specified in your will, the inheritance will be transferred to a separate trust fund and will be managed by the nominated trustee in accordance with provisions set out in your will. The trustee will continue to manage the trust property until the child in question has reached the age specified in your will. At that time, the remainder of the trust property will be transferred to the now adult beneficiary and the trust will be terminated. During the course of the trust, the trustee will have broad discretion over the management and distribution of the trust property. If the trustee deems it appropriate, he or she can release monies to or make payments on behalf of the child to cover matters relating to education, medical and general maintenance.

While court supervision is generally not required with these types of trusts, serving as a trustee can be more onerous than simply serving as a custodian under the UTMA. For example, a trustee is required to file annual income tax returns for the child trust with the IRS. Also, because the powers of the trustees of a child's trust are set out in the will itself, it will be necessary for the trustee to produce copies of the will every time he or she has to deal with a financial institution on behalf of the minor child. By contrast, given that the powers of a UTMA custodian are provided for under statute, the majority of banks and other institutions are more familiar with their terms and are more knowledgeable of the authority given to custodians under these statutes. This makes dealing with them easier.

Children's Pot Trusts

A pot trust is a good tool to use with younger children. Pot trusts are a legal device that allows you to place monies in trust to benefit two or more of your minor children. Pot trusts, however, are somewhat unique in that trust assets are made available to whichever child needs them most rather than being divided equally for the benefit of each child. With a pot trust, your trustee has discretion to apportion the trust funds between the children as he or she sees fit. So, for example, if one of your children wishes to go to college, your trustee can take a portion of the money from the trust to send that child to college. Similarly, should one of your children require an expensive medical treatment, monies can be released from the trust to cover the costs of the treatment.

A pot trust will terminate when the youngest child reaches a specified age (known as the age of termination of the trust) which is usually between 18 to 30 years of age. At that time, the trust is divided between the children equally.

One of the principal drawbacks to using a pot trust is that older children will not receive their share of the balance of the trust property until the youngest child reaches the designated age of termination of the trust. As such, they may well be into adulthood by the time they receive their shares of the inheritance.

Whom Should You Choose as a Trustee?

A trustee's duties can continue for a number of years and, in many cases, may require expertise in investing money, dealing with property, paying bills, filing accounts and managing money on behalf of the trust's underlying beneficiaries. As such, you will need to carefully consider your choice of proposed trustee. In many cases, people who establish a trust tend to choose a family member or close friend as trustee as they tend not to charge fees for carrying out the role. This is absolutely fine so long as the person is capable of handling the financial matters involved and has sufficient time to carry out the role – and of course is willing to do so… remember to check with them first!

Professional trustees, on the other hand, will charge annual management fees for providing trustee services. In some instances, these fees can be quite substantial. However, given the expertise that a professional trustee can bring to the table, it is important to at least consider engaging them where you have a large estate.

If you decide not to use a professional trustee and opt for a family member or friend instead, then the characteristics that you should look for in your nominee are honesty, intelligence, diligence and conscientiousness. Having these qualities, above all else, will at least go some way towards ensuring that you pick the right person for the job! Remember, that your trustee can always get investment advice if he or she feels it necessary or helpful!

EXECUTORS

Executors

An executor is the person named in a will to carry out the administration of the deceased's estate in accordance with the provisions of that will. If the deceased failed to make a valid will, or where there is a partial intestacy, the court will appoint a person known as an administrator to wind up the affairs of the deceased (or deal with those assets not dealt with under the will) in accordance with the intestacy laws.

When making a will, you are free to appoint anyone you wish to act as your executor provided they are an adult and of sound mind. In this regard, you can appoint a relative, a beneficiary under your will, a lawyer or even a bank or professional trustee - the choice is yours. It is also possible to appoint more than one person to act as your executor. Where more than one executor is appointed, these co-executors can act separately (each one with full authority to act on behalf of your estate) or they can be required under the terms of your will to act jointly in which case both executors (or all executors, if there are more than two) must agree to a course of action before taking that action.

Upon your death, your executor will have the legal responsibility and fiduciary duty to handle, safeguard and distribute your property in accordance with the terms of your will. In addition, your executor will also be responsible for procuring the payment of any debts or taxes owing by you or your estate at the date of your death. These debts and taxes, if any, will be paid from your estate (using the assets of the estate) before the distribution of the remainder of the estate's property to the beneficiaries named under your will.

Alternate Executors

When making your will, it's always a good idea to appoint one or more alternate executors. An alternate executor is someone who will perform the duties of the first named executor should they be unable or unwilling to do so (for whatever reason). If the alternate executor is required to act, he or she will be bound by the same legal responsibilities and fiduciary duties as the original executor.

Overview of Executors' Duties

An executor's duties will usually include locating, collecting, assessing and managing the estate's assets; arranging the discharge of debts and taxes owing by the estate; distributing cash gifts and specific item gifts in accordance with the terms of the deceased's will; and entering into appropriate contracts to effect the transfer of real property from the estate to the relevant beneficiary named under the testator's will. It is also the executor's duty to report the testator's death to insurance companies, banks, and other institutions that might owe money to or hold money on behalf of the estate.

Who Should Be Your Executor?

Choosing an executor is one of the most fundamental tasks associated with making a will. Getting the choice right can mean the difference between a smooth administration on one hand and a tardy administration with unexpected delays and costs on the other hand. It's therefore important to take your time and make the correct choice. Typically, the characteristics to look for in a good executor include good common sense, excellent organizational skills and integrity.

Of course, many people tend to choose their spouse, a sibling, an adult child or a good friend as their executor. Others choose professionals such as a lawyer, accountant or professional trustee. All are good choices provided that the person chosen is both competent and trustworthy.

Other things being equal, it will often pay to choose a family member or friend as executor for the simple reason that these people expect little (if any) compensation in return for their time, will respect your wishes, and are generally keen to progress and finalize things as quickly as possible. However, keep in mind that the process can be quite administrative and time is often of the essence. So, you should still ensure that you choose someone who is organizationally reliable and generally up to the task.

It is not enough, however, to simply appoint someone who has all the hallmarks of a good executor. You must actually appoint someone who is willing to take on the role as it is always open for a person to refuse to accept the role despite being nominated in a will. In fact, many often refuse to act as executors because they are either too busy to take on the task or feel daunted by the prospect of doing so.

If your chosen executor refuses the appointment, a court will appoint someone else to fulfill the role. Usually, this will be a relative, a beneficiary under your will or a creditor of your estate.

Once you have decided on who you would like to appoint as your executor, it's important that you actually discuss your choice with them before actually naming them in your will. You will need to explain to your proposed executor the nature of his or her role and that it may not be a straight forward and easy process. If, after explaining the role, your nominee is willing to take on the task, then you should be free to formally appoint them under your will.

Resource

For further information on executors and probate, see our book entitled "How to Probate an Estate - A Step-By-Step Guide for Executors". See page 151.

A BRIEF INTRODUCTION TO TAX

Introduction

The information below is provided as a brief overview of taxation in the United States. If you have any tax queries relating to the disposal or distribution of your estate, it is recommend that you speak to a qualified lawyer or tax advisor.

Estate Taxes

When accountants, lawyers and others who deal with these matters refer to 'estate tax' they are usually referring to federal tax, not state tax. This distinction is made for three main reasons: (i) many states do not impose an inheritance or death tax; (ii) federal tax is likely to devour more of an estate than state tax will; and (iii) reducing the federal estate tax will often result in a reduction of state taxes as well.

Estate Tax Update

Estate tax was temporarily "phased out" by the government during 2010. Until mid-December 2010, there was a degree of uncertainty as to whether estate tax would be reintroduced and, if it was, the precise manner that it would take upon reintroduction. This uncertainty came to an end on 17 December, 2010 when President Obama signed new legislation into law which extended the previous estate tax cuts introduced by the Bush administration. For the next two years (2011 and 2012), the estate tax rate has been reduced from 55% to 35% and the estate tax exemption threshold (also called a 'coupon') has been increased to $5,000,000 – up from $3,500,000 in 2009. In addition, the gift tax exemption has increased from $1,000,000 to $5,000,000.

In 2013, the estate tax exemption was raised to $5,250,000, taking inflation adjustments into consideration for the first time. The estate tax was subsequently applied at a rate of 40% on the excess. In 2014 the exemption rose yet again to $5,340,000 for an individual and $10,680,000 for a married couple. The estate tax rate of 40% is set to remain unchanged for 2014. However, that figure rose again in 2016 allocating a gift exemption of $5,450,000 to an individual and $10,900,000 to a married couple.

Federal Estate and Gift Tax

The U.S. tax system generally taxes transfers of wealth. This means the federal government usually charges a tax when money or other assets are transferred from one person to another. Keeping this general rule in mind helps to understand estate and gift taxes.

Gift tax, unlike most income taxes, is assessed on the giver, and not the receiver. As such, if you make a gift of cash or an asset to someone, you will be assessed to a gift tax unless you fall within the scope of the exceptions set out under the headings below. When gift tax is payable, you will need to record details of the gift on IRS form 709. Like many other tax forms, the gift tax form is generally due April 15th in the year following the year in which you made the gift.

Similarly, when you die, another transfer of assets takes place from you to someone else. Like the gift tax, the estate tax is imposed on the giver, which in that case will be your estate. A federal estate tax return is reported on IRS form 706, and is due to be filed with the IRS within nine months of the date of your death unless extended.

Everyone's "Coupon"

The gift and estate tax have to be considered together, because they are intertwined in that both are taken into account when calculating the maximum amount that you can give away or, if you die, your estate can transfer without incurring a charge to tax. Simply speaking, the maximum amount you can transfer without incurring gift or estate tax is like a "coupon". When the value of your gifts and estate are calculated, you can apply this "coupon" to minimize or avoid the tax. You will only have to pay gift or estate tax if your gifts and/or transfers exceed this "coupon" amount.

For 2016, the "coupon" for gifts and estates (i.e. the "exclusion amount") is $5.45 million. That means that you can transfer up to $5.45 million in gifts during your lifetime to anyone you choose and there won't be any gift tax due. However, if you exceed the value of the "coupon", you'll owe tax on the excess gift(s). Under current law, the rate of gift tax varies based on the year of the gift. A chart detailing the rate of gift and estate tax can be found under the heading "How to Determine the Estate Tax".

For example, if you give $2,000,000 of taxable gifts to each of your three children over your lifetime, you'll have made $6,000,000 in taxable gifts. You can use your "coupon" to avoid tax on the first $5,450,000, but you'll owe tax on the other $550,000.

How does this relate to estate taxes? Well, for most years, you also have a "coupon" for estate taxes. However, as the government views every dollar you gave away during your lifetime as a dollar less that can be taxed in your estate when you die, this "coupon" will be reduced by the amount of the gift tax "coupon" that you have used during your lifetime! So, while there is also a "coupon" for estate tax, it is linked to the gift tax "coupon"; and more specifically to the amount of that gift tax "coupon" that you have already used.

Let's say you made those three $2,000,000 gifts to your children and still had $7.34 million in your taxable estate when you died in 2016, when the estate tax "coupon" is $5.45 million. Because you used the full $5.45 million gift tax "coupon" during your lifetime, your estate tax "coupon" is reduced by $5.45 million to $0, and estate tax will be owed on the entire value of your estate.

If, on the other hand, if you had only given each or your children $250,000 during your lifetime and thereby only used $750,000 of your "coupon," your estate tax "coupon" would be $4.70 million ($5,450,000 less $750,000). Therefore, estate tax would only be owed on $2,640,000 of your estate ($7.34 million total value of the estate less the $4.70 million remaining on the "coupon").

Your estate tax "coupon" is reduced by any gift tax "coupon" that you have already used. On the other hand, if you had used only $500,000 of your gift tax "coupon", your estate tax "coupon" would be $4.95 million ($5,450,000 estate tax "coupon" less $500,000 of gift tax "coupon" used).

Example: *Margot gave Rick and John a total of $4 million during her lifetime that used up most of her lifetime gifting exemption of $5.45 million. Margot died in 2016. The estate tax threshold in 2016 was $5.45 million. However, in order to determine whether Margot had reached her estate tax exemption threshold, the gifts she made during her lifetime will be taken into account. As such, on her death, her exemption would only be $1.45 million ($5.45 million less the $4 million gift tax exemption used).*

What Is the "Coupon" Amount?

As the chart below shows, both the gift tax and estate tax "coupons" are each currently set at $5 million having increased substantially over the last few years.

Year of Gift or Death	Gift Tax Coupon	Estate Tax Coupon
2011 and 2012	$5,000,000	$5,000,000
2013	$5,250,000	$5,250,000
2014	$5,340,000	$5,340,000
2015	$5,430,000	$5,430,000
2016	$5,450,000	$5,450,000

How to Determine the Estate Tax?

The first question to ask when trying to determine the amount of federal estate tax which might be due by your estate is "What is the fair market value of everything you own, control, or have an interest in at the date of your death?" In answering this question, you will need to include all assets you own such as cash, investments, real estate, and personal property such as cars, boats, art and the like. Estate tax is also levied on the life insurance policies in your name where you have a right of ownership in the policy.

The total value of all of these items is called your "gross estate". Your taxable estate is your gross estate less certain deductions. These deductions may include mortgages on your assets, debts you owe, estate administration expenses, property that passes automatically to your surviving spouse, and bequests to qualified charities (more on the deductions for spouses and charities below). The value of your gross estate minus these deductions is referred to as your "taxable estate".

Once you have calculated your taxable estate, estate tax may be owed if the value of the taxable estate exceeds the unused portion of your estate tax "coupon."

Just as the value of the "coupon" changes depending on the year in which you make a gift or die, the percentage of the tax assessment also changes.

Year of Gift/Death	Maximum Gift Tax	Maximum Estate Tax
2010	35%	N/A
2011 and 2012	35%	35$
2013 and 2014	40%	40%

Year of Gift/Death	Maximum Gift Tax	Maximum Estate Tax
2015 and 2016	40%	40%

State Taxes

Not every state imposes a separate state tax on estates or inheritances. Florida, for instance, imposes no state death tax. Where there is such a tax, it is likely to be one (or a combination) of three types of tax: (1) death tax, (2) inheritance tax, or (3) pick-up tax.

State Death Taxes

Generally, when people use the phrase "death tax", they are referring to state taxes levied on an estate upon death. The amount of state tax due, if any, is determined on a state-by-state basis according to that state's tax laws and is often calculated in a manner similar to federal estate tax.

State Inheritance Taxes

In states with inheritance tax laws, inheritance tax is paid by the person who receives assets either under a will or on intestacy. As with intestacy laws, beneficiaries are divided into different classes based on the closeness or remoteness of their relationship to the deceased. One tax rate may apply to all assets in the estate, or the rate may vary depending upon who receives what property. Generally speaking the closer the person receiving a gift from the deceased is to the deceased (in terms of blood line), the lower the tax rate on the transfer of property to that person. Thus, depending on what class the beneficiary falls into, he or she will be taxed at a specific rate.

INHERITANCE TAX STATES			
State	Tax Rate	State	Tax Rate
Iowa	5%-15%	Nebraska	1%-18%
Kentucky	6%-16%	New Jersey	11%-16%
Maryland	10%	Pennsylvania	4.5%-15%

State "Pick-Up" Taxes

Some states base all or a portion of their state death tax on the amount of credit that the federal estate tax used to allow for state death taxes. Prior to 2005, federal estate taxes could be reduced by a credit for the amount of state death taxes paid. The result was that the federal estate tax was a "maximum" tax that was paid partly to the state and partly to the federal government. Many states therefore would "pick-up" their tax revenue by pegging their state death taxes at the amount of the federal credit that you could claim for state death taxes. After 2001, the federal government gradually eliminated the credit for state death taxes. However, some states chose to continue to charge a pick-up tax based on what the federal credit was in 2001, even though the federal credit is no longer available.

For all three of the types of tax a state might assess, some states will have a "coupon" equal to the federal tax "coupon", meaning that if there is no federal estate tax there is no state estate tax. However, many states have chosen not to increase their "coupons" at the same rate that the federal law does, so the state "coupon" may be smaller, resulting in state estate tax even where there is no federal estate tax.

Marital Deduction

Remember the gift and estate tax "coupon" for federal taxes? Historically, it was unique to each individual/estate and could not be used by anyone else. That meant that you had a "coupon" and your spouse had a "coupon" and they were non-transferable.

The "coupons" are not used up by gifts made or estates transferred to a spouse who is a U.S. citizen. Instead, federal gift/estate tax applies an unlimited deduction to those transfers. In other words, you can gift or transfer an unlimited amount of property to your U.S. citizen spouse and there is no gift or estate tax on that transfer.

That's the good news. The bad news is that the marital deduction is, in some ways, just a waiting game whereby the government allows you to transfer your property tax free to your spouse with the view that it will later be taxed when your spouse dies or gives it away. As your spouse could not use your gift/estate tax "coupon" prior to the introduction of the Tax Relief, Unemployment Insurance Reauthorization, and Job Creation Act of 2010, in December 2010, that meant that your spouse had more to transfer to her beneficiaries and heirs but without the benefit of an increased "coupon". However, in December 2010, President Obama signed this legislation into law which entitled a person to use any unused element of his or her deceased spouse's coupon. However, that right would be lost if the surviving spouse remarried!

Consider this example: Your last will & testament provides for your spouse to inherit everything you own when you die. At your death, your net taxable estate is $6,000,000 and your spouse also has an estate worth $6,000,000 (a combined net worth of $12,000,000). Since your spouse was the recipient of your estate, the unlimited marital deduction applies and there is no estate tax due as a result of your death regardless of the applicable "coupon". If your spouse dies in 2016, under current law your spouse's maximum "coupon" will be $10,900,000 - ($5,450,000 of his or her own plus $5,450,000 of yours) assuming neither of you previously used any element of your coupon. Of course, to the extent that either of you used your coupon, this amount will be deducted from the $10,900,000 coupon. Ultimately, your spouse's estate will be subject to tax on the excess of $1,100,000. At a tax rate of 40%, that translates to a tax of $440,000.

Important Note

A surviving spouse will lose the right to use his or her deceased spouse's coupon if he or she remarries!

Non-Citizen Spouses

The unlimited marital deduction is available only when you give or leave your assets to a spouse who is a U.S. citizen at the time the transfer is made. Some types of credit shelter trust planning mechanisms are also only effective if your spouse is a U.S. citizen. If your spouse is not a citizen, your estate plan must include more sophisticated trust planning designed to keep the assets in the United States managed by a U.S. trustee so that the trust can qualify for the marital deduction that is otherwise only available to U.S. citizen spouses. This is called a Qualified Domestic Trust, or QDOT. For more information, speak to your attorney

Other Ways to Reduce Estate Taxes

Federal estate tax can be reduced through a variety of other legitimate estate planning techniques. Since the "coupon" has increased to $5.45 million per person, those with large estates over this amount could benefit from considering some of the methods listed below to reduce potential estate tax liability. The advantages and disadvantages of these techniques vary greatly depending on the individual circumstances of the persons using them. That is why having an experienced attorney or tax advisor can be beneficial as you consider how these techniques fit your particular situation.

Lifetime Gifts

Under federal tax law, some gifts incur no gift tax, don't require filing of a gift tax return, and don't even use up any of your "coupon." For example, in 2016 you may make an annual tax exempt gift to any one person provided the total amount of gifts to that person during the calendar year does not exceed $14,000. This exemption applies to each person making a gift which means that if both you and your spouse utilize this estate planning tool, you could collectively reduce your estate by giving away $28,000 a year to any number of beneficiaries, free of any federal gift tax. The annual exemption amount changes based on inflation, but over a period of several years the amount of money that you and your spouse (or partner) could transfer to your intended beneficiaries under this method could be quite substantial.

You can also make tax-free gifts by paying someone's medical expenses or tuition bills provided that you pay the bill directly to the medical or educational institution. Gifts of this type are not subject to the annual exemption limits and can be in any amount.

Making lifetime gifts as described above removes the gifted assets from your estate, potentially reducing the amount your estate would otherwise have to pay in federal estate tax. However, during most years, lifetime gifts may be less advantageous than inheritances when we consider the effect of capital gains taxes. Capital gain is the amount you get when you sell the asset minus your basis. Broadly speaking, basis is the amount you have invested in the asset. So, if you sell an asset for $100 where your basis was $10, you will have a capital gain of $90 that is subject to capital gains tax. When you make a gift during your lifetime, the recipient of the gift has the same basis in the gifted asset as you have. As a result, the $100 asset will have the same $90 capital gain when the recipient sells it as you would have incurred if you had sold it. The transfer of the initial $10 basis to the recipient in this manner is referred to as a "carry-over basis".

However, in most years if you leave the asset as an inheritance rather than a lifetime gift, your recipient now gets a "stepped up basis" to the value of the asset on the date that you died. In the case of our $100 asset, if the value was $100 when you died, the recipient would now have a basis of $100 (rather than a carry-over basis of $10). If the recipient sells the asset for $100, there will be no capital gains subject to tax. Since capital gains taxes are currently around 15%, gifting the asset would have cost the recipient $13.50 in capital gains tax ($90 x .15) while inheriting the asset wouldn't have incurred any tax. This difference in basis is why it is important to consult a tax advisor before making significant lifetime gifts as part of your estate planning.

Let's consider another example using the "stepped up basis". You have just inherited a house from your father. The house originally purchased by your father, 40 years ago for the sum of $40,000. You have decided to sell the house and have recently made the house available for sale on the market. The house sells for $400,000. The difference between the purchasing and selling price is $360,000, which would normally require capital gains to be paid to that amount, which could range in the region of 20%, resulting in a $72,000 taxation fee. Of course this rate could be less depending on the length of time you have owned the house, your income and several other factors prior to its sale.

Let's consider the same information, but from a different viewpoint. This time we will focus on how the "Stepped up basis" works. Let's assume that the market value of the house was $360,000 on the date of your father's death. Under the stepped up approach your capital gains tax would be significant different. The taxable amount would be $400,000 - $360,000 leaving you with a capital gains payment on the $40,000 profit.

There are several things worth considering when faced with the inheritance of a house. Firstly, capital gains tax treat long-term and short-term ownership differently, which could have a very different tax outcome. Depending on your personal income, if you sell the house within two years of inheritance you could be liable up to between 15%- 28% of the gain in 2016. On the other hand if you are single and decide to hold the property for two years or more, make the property your principle residence, then you could be looking of a capital gain exemption of up to $250,000. Together with the stepped up basis show above in relation to your father of $360,000, you could avoid any tax liability.

Of course, another scenario could arise, one which sees you selling the house for less than the stepped-up basis, in such case you will have a capital loss. In the event that you do find yourself with a capital loss and you don't use the residence as your personal residence, $3,000 of the loss can be deducted against your ordinary income per year. Any amounts over $3,000 can be carried over for subsequent years.

In addition, as a married couple you may be entitled to double the exemption amount of $250,000 allocated for a single person and claim a total combined exemption of $500,000.

Based on the various examples and scenarios above, you can see the benefit of getting tax advice to help with your estate planning. While the above does provide an insight into some tax issues, a tax consultant will be able to provide advice specific to your situation.

Irrevocable Life Insurance Trusts

An irrevocable life insurance trust creates a trust that is used exclusively to own life insurance. The trust purchases life insurance on your life, and you make gifts to the trust to pay the premiums. The trust may not be revoked and once you place funds into the trust, they cannot be taken back. Upon your death, the life insurance payout is distributed according to the terms of the trust. Because you do not control the life insurance, it is not considered part of your taxable estate and thus no federal estate taxes are due when the payout is made.

Family Limited Partnerships

A family limited partnership helps families transfer ownership of their closely-held businesses to the next generation of business managers. A family limited partnership, or FLP, is created to hold and manage assets. You may transfer those assets to the FLP in exchange for your interest in the partnership. You then gift some of your partnership interest to your children, perhaps over a number of years. FLPs can save estate taxes in two ways. First, they can remove from your estate now assets that are likely to appreciate. Even though the asset is removed from the estate, you may retain control over the partnership and therefore have continued control over how the asset is managed. Second, the percentage gift you make to an FLP may be valued at less than the same percentage of the value of the assets in the partnership.

For example, assume you establish a partnership with three pieces of real estate each valued at $500,000. The value of the assets in the partnership total $1,500,000. Then you gift a ten percent interest in the partnership to your son. While ten percent of the value of the partnership assets is $150,000 ($1,500,000 x .10), the value of a ten percent interest in the partnership may be appreciably less than $150,000. This is because as a ten percent owner your son doesn't have control over the assets and there isn't likely to be someone willing to pay him $150,000 for the chance to be a minority partner that lacks control.

Conclusion

Estate taxes and estate tax planning are complicated areas of the law. If you have an estate greater than five million dollars or have other special circumstances, we recommend that you seek professional advice before employing any of the tax reduction strategies outlined in this section.

GETTING READY TO MAKE YOUR OWN WILL!

Do I Need a Lawyer?

The short answer is "no". You are free to draft your own will without hiring a lawyer or legal advisor. If your situation is not a complicated one, and you simply want to make gifts, appoint guardians and executors etc under your will, then preparing your own will should not be very difficult provided that you have some good self-help materials to hand. However, if your situation is complex or is unusual in some way, you should, at the very least, consult a lawyer.

Deciding on Your Beneficiaries

The first thing you need to do when making a will is to make some lists. You will need to list some or all of the following items:-

- your objectives in distributing your estate;

- your assets and liabilities;

- family members whom you wish to benefit under your will;

- friends and others that you would like to benefit under your will – maybe you want to make a gift to your faithful housekeeper of many years or the friend who's stood by you through all your highs and lows, for example;

- the relationship between you and each of the beneficiaries (this helps for identification purposes);

- charities that you wish to make a gift to; and

- list the particular items, or cash amounts, that you want each beneficiary to receive.

Once you have made your lists and decided on who is to receive cash or specific gifts, you should also consider the balance or residuary of your estate. Do this, even if you think you've distributed everything you possess already. Decide on who will receive that and, if more than one person, the percentage share that each will receive.

To help you make the above lists, we have included a Will Writing Worksheet at the back of this kit. You can write on the pages in this kit or, alternatively, download the form directly from www.enodare.com.

Once you have decided on the people and organizations that will receive your assets, the next step will be for you to decide on who will act as your executors.

Deciding on Who to Appoint as Your Executors

Unless your estate is very large and complex, two people will be sufficient to act as the executors of your estate. A spouse, son, daughter or other close family member is usually the best place to start when choosing an executor, or failing any of them being willing or suitable, a close and trusted friend. The second executor/executrix might be another son or daughter, your (preferably younger) sibling, or your lawyer or accountant.

Again, before appointing an executor, be sure to ask whether they would be willing and able to take on the role.

Deciding on Who to Appoint as Guardians of Your Minor Children

If you have minor children you should appoint a guardian for your children – even if your spouse is still alive. The clause will say something like "If my wife Mary (or "husband John") predeceases me then I appoint John Smith as testamentary guardian of my minor children". Keep in mind that the guardian you appoint must be an adult. In practice, it's common to appoint one's brother or sister and their spouse to take on this role together, provided they are willing and able to do so. In the case of a young family, the children's grandparents might be a natural choice for guardians.

Deciding What Type of Will You Need

Review the descriptions of the wills at the start of Appendix 3 and choose the will which best describes your circumstances. Then print your chosen will and complete it in accordance with the instructions in Appendix 4 and Appendix 5. (or download a copy to your computer and complete it).

Choosing People to Witness You Signing Your Will

The laws in most states provide that in order for a will to be valid two people must witness the testator sign the will. In Vermont three witnesses are required. In order for a person to act as a witness to the testator's signing of the will, they must have reached the age of majority in the the testator's state of residence and should not be a beneficiary under the will (or the spouse or civil partner of any such beneficiary). If a beneficiary under a will (or their spouse or civil partner for that matter) acts as a witness then the gift to the beneficiary will be deemed to be void. The will, however, will otherwise remain valid.

Singing Your Will

The laws of each state set out the formal requirements for executing a will. In general, your will must be executed in the following manner:-

- you must first (in the presence of witnesses) sign your name, using a pen, in the space provided for signature on the final page of your will; and

- each of your chosen witnesses must then, in your presence and in the presence of each other, write his/her name, address and occupation in the space provided on the final page of the will and also sign their name with their normal signature.

 Did You Know?

Generally, a will must be signed by you or by someone directed to do so on your behalf. Signatures may include marks, initials, a rubber stamp, a 'nick-name' or even a former name.

AFTER YOU HAVE MADE YOUR WILL....

Where to Store Your Will

Once your will has been properly executed, place it in a safe place that is accessible to your executors after your death. Make sure a close friend, relative or your executor knows where to find your will and how to get access to it when the time comes. If you had a lawyer prepare your will, it would be useful to have him or her retain the original in their strong room or safe, or even retain a copy with a note stating where the original can be found!

Just don't be too clever! The last thing you want is a will hunt, especially if you have made and revoked a number of wills, and no one is sure of the date of your most recent one!

Resource

We also recommend that you use the online storage facilities such as those offered by Legal Vault™. Legal Vaults™ is a relatively unique service that allows people to store estate planning, medical and other important documents and information online. The information and documents can be accessed in whole or in part by people to whom you have provided the security codes. The use of this highly recommended service ensures that your documents are always to hand when needed. For further information on Legal Vaults™ visit www.legalvault.com.

Keeping Your Will Updated

In drafting your will, it's important to understand that events will most likely occur in your lifetime which will give rise to a need to change the provisions of your will. These events may come around as a result of changes in the law, your financial circumstances, the value of your assets and even in your preferences in relation to beneficiaries. If your will is not updated to address these changes, they can have significant unintended consequences – particularly in respect of the manner in which your assets are ultimately divided amongst your family and friends.

Some typical changes in circumstances that can cause unintended consequences if not addressed include:

- birth of new family members;

- death of intended beneficiaries;

- significant changes in beneficiaries' circumstances;

- changes in your relationships (such as marriage or divorce);

- acquisition of new assets;

- substantial appreciation in value of particular existing assets; and

- disposal or substantial depreciation in value or loss of certain existing assets.

Important Note

Changes in your circumstances can affect your distribution plans!! Perhaps,

- you remarried and 'inherited' a new stepchild or two. Yet neither your new spouse nor your stepchildren are mentioned in your will.

- you left various blocks of shares to different children. One block has more than doubled in value, while another is practically worthless with the primary company in the portfolio going into liquidation. Yet you meant your children to share more or less equally.

- a small parcel of land you left to your cousin has suddenly quadrupled in price due to a new shopping centre project getting the go–ahead. The value of their inheritance may be far more than you intended to leave them.

- you sold a valuable painting you had earmarked for one of your grandchildren? Unless you substitute a different bequest, that grandchild might end up inheriting nothing.

Suddenly your bequests are way out of balance. If this happens, it's time to update your will!

In order to make sure that changes in your circumstances are addressed in your will it is recommended that you review and update your will annually or at the very least, every three years. It's also recommended that you review your will on the occurrence of any significant change in your personal circumstances such as in the cases of the examples set out above.

Using a Codicil to Update or Change Your Will

You are free to change the terms of your will including the beneficiaries named in it whenever you like. Of course, you do need to be careful when dealing with spouses due to their legal rights. Fortunately, amending your will is relatively straightforward. To amend a will, you can either make a new will in its entirety or you can make a codicil which will amend a specific portion of your existing will.

A codicil is simply a testamentary document that amends rather than replaces an existing will. It requires exactly the same formalities as to execution as does a will. You can use different witnesses, but it's better (if they can be easily found) to use the same people who witnessed the original will. Once the codicil has been executed, it should be placed with the original will for safe keeping.

Similar to the position with wills, a witness to a codicil should not be a beneficiary under the codicil, as this will preclude them from inheriting under the codicil.

 Resource

Full details on how to prepare a codicil are contained in our kit entitled "Codicil to Will Kit". For your immediate copy, simply visit www.enodare.com.

Revoking Your Will

If you need to revoke your will for any reason, you may do so in several ways:

- draft a new will (which will usually contain a statement that all old wills are revoked);

- physically destroy your old will by tearing it up or burning it;

- a will can be revoked by marriage or the signing of a civil partnership agreement unless your will was drafted "in contemplation of marriage" or "in contemplation of the civil partnership"; and

- where you have a child after signing the will, your will may be revoked if you have not dealt with this possibility in your will.

 Warning

Note: The writing of the word 'revoked' on a will is insufficient to legally revoke the will.

For the avoidance of doubt, you should always consider updating your will after you divorce or separate from your partner.

DEALING WITH DIGITAL ASSETS

Preparing a Digital Plan

Take a minute and think about how much of your life is performed and managed using a computer, a tablet, and/or a cell phone. The possibilities in today's technological age are vast: bank statements and account transactions; credit card statements, transactions and payments; investment accounts and transactions; e-mail accounts; social media such as Facebook and Twitter; digital storage facilities such as Flickr and Amazon Cloud; etc. Now imagine what would happen if you unexpectedly died or became incapacitated. Even if you have taken the steps of naming a capable executor and/or trustee, and of granting a trusted person a durable power of attorney to manage your financial and personal affairs, do these persons have the information necessary to access your digital accounts? Would they know how to sort through the contents of these accounts even if they did have access information?

For example, do your executor, trustee and agent have access to a list of all of your passwords to all of your digital accounts? Do they have instructions on how to manage your digital accounts? If not, you could place them in an administrative and logistical nightmare attempting to unlock these accounts in order to perform their assigned tasks and protect your assets and estate. Bills could go unpaid, funds unmanaged, etc. until the person handling your affairs can produce the proper documents to the court and appropriate institutions that allows them the access and control they need.

This is why in the modern age of digital technology, almost everyone's estate plan should include a plan for handling financial and social digital accounts. This digital estate plan should include:

- An inventory of digital assets and passwords

- Secure storage of passwords

- Selection of a digital guardian/executor

- Access to passwords

- Clear instructions on how to handle digital accounts

Creating a Digital Inventory

You should create a detailed list of all of your digital accounts, along with their passwords and security question answers. The importance of preparing and maintaining this inventory cannot be overstated, because it may be impossible for executors, other fiduciaries, and family members to discover many digital assets if they don't even know these assets exist and where to look for them. For security purposes, you may want to make two lists—one with the account numbers and one with the passwords and security question answers.

Your financial digital inventory should include the following:

- Bank accounts that you access online

- Brokerage accounts that you access online

- Retirement plan accounts that you access online

- Insurance plan accounts that you access online

- Credit card accounts that you access online

- Online retail accounts and digital wallet accounts

- Online sales accounts

- PayPal or other online payment accounts

- Utility bills and other services for which you pay online

- Tax information in digital form

- Business websites

- Business e-mail accounts

Your social digital inventory should include the following:

- Personal e-mail accounts

- Social media accounts such as Facebook, Twitter, and LinkedIn

- Data and document storage accounts like Drop-Box or Google Docs

- Personal websites

- Photo-sharing sites like Flickr or video-sharing sites like YouTube

- Music sites like Pandora

In addition, you should inventory all of your personal computers, laptop computers, tablets, and cell phones.

Make sure you update your digital inventory whenever you change an important password, and in any event as often as possible.

Storage of Your Digital Assets

Once you've created a digital inventory, the next step is to find a secure place to keep this vital information, which could lead to identity theft if obtained by the wrong person. Fortunately, new businesses are springing up to meet the modern digital challenges, including companies providing secure data storage. The key is to find a system that meets your strict security requirements and matches your technological capabilities in order to ensure that you actually use the system you select. One place not to put this information is in your will, because after you die this becomes a public document.

The options you do have for storing your digital account information and passwords include online storage accounts, password-protected electronic files, and old-fashioned methods such as a home safe.

Online Storage Accounts

Companies now offer services to allow users to store digital account information and passwords, as well as documents such as your wills and trusts, using state-of-the-art security for a monthly or yearly fee. Upon your death or incapacity, a person you designate is allowed immediate access to the online storage account and is able to obtain the digital information they need to manage your affairs. Remember, the information held in the online storage account must be accurate and up-to-date for the service to work as intended.

Currently popular online storage accounts include legacylocker.com and secureasafe.com. Do some research before choosing an online storage company. Most of these companies are new and therefore there is no guarantee that the one you choose will not go out of business. Also make sure their security and encryption systems are up to industry standards. Check that the connection between their system and your device is encrypted. This prevents interception while the data is being transmitted. Then be sure the data is also encrypted. No one should be able to unlock it without your password.

If you decide to use an online storage account to secure digital assets and information, you need to tell someone that the account exists. If you are not comfortable disclosing the existence of the online storage during your lifetime to the person who will have access upon your death or incapacity, then give the information to another fiduciary or very trusted family member or friend.

Password-protected Flash Drive or Computer File

You can keep your digital asset inventory on a USB flash drive or computer file, but to be secure the file in which the inventory resides should be encrypted with a complex password. The best way to do this is to use a software package designed to store confidential documents and passwords, such as KeePass, SecuBox, or Web Confidential. The password to access the electronic list may be stored with original estate planning documents or in a safe-deposit box. Again, it is critical that this password be kept up-to-date. If a user changes the password and fails to replace the outdated password, the person designated to access the inventory will be unable to do so.

Old Fashioned Methods

If you are not comfortable with technology, or you trust an individual more than you trust online security systems, you can always do it the old-school way of putting your list in a fireproof home safe or safety deposit box at your bank. Or you can give a copy of the list to a trusted person like your spouse, child, best friend, or executor and make sure they keep it in a safe location as well. In any event, you need to guarantee someone knows the list exists, where it is located, and has the means to recover it.

Choosing a Digital Executor

Once you have created and properly stored your digital inventory, you need to select someone to have access to your digital accounts should you die or become incapacitated. This may well be the same person who is the executor of your entire estate, the trustee of your trusts, or the agent named in your general durable power of attorney. However, you need to make sure this person is technologically acute enough to handle the job of managing your digital assets, and if not find someone who is and name them as co-executor, co-trustee, or co-agent for the specific purpose of managing your digital estate. Then you need to provide this person with the access information and detailed instructions necessary to do so.

Providing Instructions for Digital Assets

While your estate plan should already describe what should happen to the assets contained in your digital accounts upon your death, you need to provide a road map to these accounts and specific instructions as to how to manage them, both to your executor and successor trustee upon your death, and any of your agents and alternate trustees upon your incapacity. This could be as simple as describing an automatic monthly credit card payment, or as complicated as a web of brokerage and investment accounts with supporting computer files.

In addition, you need to provide detailed instructions on how you want your e-mail accounts and social digital assets, such as Facebook and Twitter, handled. In doing so, however, it is very important that you review the terms and conditions of each of these accounts, because federal and state laws criminalize certain types of unauthorized access to computers or data. This means that if your executor or agent is not authorized to access one of your e-mail or other accounts under the provider's terms of service, then doing so could be a crime even if you expressly authorized access and provided the passwords.

Most social media services, including Facebook, MySpace, Twitter, and LinkedIn, do not allow an assignment or transfer of a user's account. Therefore, your executor's choices for your social media accounts are to either request the deactivation or deletion of the account, or leave the account as is.

Should you wish to complete a digital estate plan, a blank form is contained in Appendix 10 of this kit.

APPENDIX 1

GLOSSARY OF LEGAL TERMS

APPENDIX 1

GLOSSARY OF LEGAL TERMS

This glossary is designed to help you understand some of the more common legal terms you may encounter when making your will.

Term	Definition
Administration	The process by which an administrator oversees the distribution of your estate and deals with the payment of any outstanding debts owing by you if you die intestate.
Administrator	This is the person who is designated by the courts to oversee the administration.
Adult	This is a person which has reached the age of majority in his or her state.
Assets	All possessions of yours including insurance policies and rights to receive other assets/money.
Beneficiary	A person or organization who will inherit part or all of your assets or estate under a will, trust or on intestacy.
Bequest	A gift of personal property under a will.
Children	The term extends to include legitimate, illegitimate and adopted children. Stepchildren are often excluded from the meaning of this term and should therefore, for the avoidance of doubt, be expressly mentioned in your will or trust if you wish them to benefit.
Codicil	A codicil acts to make an amendment to your will and is legally binding once all legal formalities have been complied with.
Deceased/Decedent	The person who has died.

Term	Definition
Devise	This is a gift of immovable property (also known as real property) such as land or buildings made under a will.
Disinherit	To exclude someone who is rightfully entitled to inherit something from your estate from an inheritance.
Estate	The term "estate" refers to everything you own at the time of your death – all assets, real and personal, less your liabilities.
Executor/ Executrix	This is the person or persons nominated or appointed by you in your will to deal with the administration and distribution of your estate following your death. Executor is the masculine term whereas executrix is the feminine term. Sometimes, executors are called personal representatives.
Fiduciary	A fiduciary is someone who has undertaken to act for and on behalf of another person in a particular matter in circumstances which give rise to a relationship of trust and confidence. Examples include trustees, executors, and guardians.
Fiduciary Duty	Fiduciary duties are duties that the executor or trustee owes to the beneficiaries of the estate whose assets the executor or trustee has control over. These duties include a duty to act in good faith for the benefit of the beneficiaries.
Gift	A gift or a present is the transfer of something without the need for compensation and without any obligation on the part of the donor to make the gift.
Guardian	A legal guardian is a person who has the legal authority (and the corresponding duty) to care for the personal and property interests of a minor or an incapacitated person. In the case of minors, you can appoint a guardian under your will to care for your children following your death. However, this appointment must ultimately be approved by the court.

Term	Definition
Heir	A person who is entitled either by law or by the terms of a will or trust to inherit the estate of another.
Inherit	To receive something, by legal succession or bequest, after the previous owner's death.
Intestate/Intestacy	Where you die without making a valid will to deal with the distribution of your estate you are said to have died intestate. Where this happens, intestacy proceedings will be instituted whereby the court will appoint an administrator to distribute your estate and pay your debts in accordance with the law. These laws are known as the rules of 'intestacy'.
Intestate Succession	The order in which people inherit property when someone dies intestate.
Issue	The immediate descendants of a person.
Legacy	A gift made in a will.
Minor	A child who has not yet reached the age of majority.
Per stirpes	A "per stirpes" arrangement means that if a beneficiary/heir predeceases the testator/intestate leaving a child then that child takes the share that his parent would have been entitled to receive had the parent been alive. Where there is more than one child, that share is divided equally amongst the children.
Personal Property	Physical assets that are not fixed permanently to real estate. It includes mobile property like furniture, equipment, vehicles, collectibles and inventory for example.
Personal Representative	Another name for an executor.

Term	Definition
Primary Beneficiary	This is the person who stands first in line to receive a gift under a will or trust. Should the primary beneficiary die before becoming entitled to receive a gift under a will or trust, the gift will pass to an alternate beneficiary (if one is named) or revert to the residuary beneficiary if no alternate is named.
Probate	Probate has come to mean not just proving the validity of a last will and testament but the entire administrative process involving the collecting of assets, payment of debts and the passing of a deceased person's legal title to property to his or her beneficiaries. If the deceased person has not made a will, this process will be known as an administration rather than a probate.
Residue/Remainder	The remainder of a testator's estate after all specific gifts have been made under the testator's will, and after all of the testator's debts have been paid.
Residuary Beneficiary	The person who will receive the residue of the testator's estate. The residue can also be divided between more than one person.
Real Property	Land and generally whatever is erected upon or affixed to it.
Spouse	A person who is married - not a cohabite.
Surviving Spouse	The husband or wife that remains alive after the death of the other spouse.
Survivorship	The right of a person to secure ownership of an asset (such as land, real estate, bank accounts etc.) by reason of the fact that this person has outlived the other joint owners.
Testamentary Trust	A trust created under the terms of a will.
Testate	A person who has died leaving a valid will providing for the distribution of his assets.

Term	Definition
Testator/Testatrix	This means the man/woman who makes a will.
Trust	A trust is a relationship of reliance whereby one party requests another party to manage property on his or her behalf, or on behalf of another in accordance with a specific set of rules. The persons who are charged with the management of the property are known as trustees.
Trustee	The person or persons who have been appointed to look after property that is held in trust. The trustees are not allowed to do anything with the property unless the terms of the trust allow it. The trustees owe a number of fiduciary duties to the beneficiaries of the trust property concerned.
Will	A legal document setting out a person's wishes regarding the disposal of his or her property after death.

APPENDIX 2

WILL WRITING WORKSHEET

Downloadable Forms

Blank copies of this form are available to download from our website.

Web: https://www.enodare.com/downloadarea/

Unlock Code: LWL20153

Appendix 2

WILL WRITING WORKSHEET

www.enodare.com

WILL WRITING WORKSHEET

Before you begin the process of making a will, we recommend that you print out this worksheet and complete it as appropriate. It will help you to work out what assets you actually own, and identify your liabilities, before deciding who you would like to make gifts to and how. By having all the relevant details at your fingertips it will save a considerable amount of time in the preparation of your estate planning documents.

The document is also useful for documenting your choice of fiduciaries such as executors, trustees, healthcare agents etc.

In addition, by keeping this worksheet with your will and other personal papers, it will greatly assist your executor in identifying and locating your assets and liabilities when the time comes.

Personal Information	You	Your Spouse
Full Name:		
Birth Date:		
Social Security Number:		
Occupation:		
Work Telephone:		
Work Fax:		
Mobile/Pager:		
Email Address:		
Home Address (Include County):		
Home Telephone:		
Home Fax:		
Date and Place of Marriage:		
Maiden Name of Spouse:		
If either of you were previously married, list the dates of prior marriage, name of previous spouse, names of living children from prior marriage(s), and state whether marriage ended by death or divorce:		
Location of Safe Deposit Box (if any):		

Notification of Death

(On my death, please notify the following persons)

Full Name	Telephone	Address

Children (Living)

Full Name	Address (If child does not reside with you)	Birth Date

Children (Deceased)

Full Name		

Grandchildren

Full Name	Address	Birth Date

Parents

Full Name	Address	Telephone Number

Brothers and Sisters		
Full Name	Address	Telephone Number

Assets		
Description & Location	Current Fair Market Value	How is Title Held?
Real Estate (Land and Buildings)		
Closely Held Companies, Businesses, Partnerships etc.		
Bank Accounts		

Shares, Bonds and Mutual Funds		
Vehicles, Boats, etc		
Other Property		
Total		

Liabilities	
Description	**Amount**
Mortgages	
Loans	
Debts	

Other Liabilities	
Total	

Life Insurance and Annuities

Company	Insured	Beneficiary(ies)	Face Amount	Cash Value
Total				

Pensions and Other Retirement Plans

Company Custodian	Participant	Type of Plan	Vested Amount	Death Benefit
Total				

Distribution Plan
(Describe in general terms how you wish to leave your property at death)

Other Beneficiaries
(Information about persons other than your spouse and family members who you wish to benefit)

Full Name	Age	Address	Relationship to You

Fiduciaries
(List name, address and home telephone for each person)

	Full Name	Address	Telephone Number
Last Will and Testament			
Primary Executor			
First Alternate Executor			
Second Alternate Executor			
Primary Trustee:			
First Alternate Trustee			
Second Alternate Trustee			
Guardian of Minor Children:			
First Alternate Guardian			
Second Alternate Guardian			
Family Trust			
Successor Trustee			
First Alternate Successor Trustee			
Second Alternate Successor Trustee			
Agent under a Power of Attorney for Finance and Property (Enduring Power of Attorney)			
Agent			
First Alternate Agent			
Second Alternate Agent			
Agent under a Healthcare Power of Attorney (Healthcare)			
Healthcare Agent			
First Alternate Healthcare Agent			
Second Alternate Healthcare Agent			

Living Will			
Healthcare Agent			
First Alternate Healthcare Agent			
Second Alternate Healthcare Agent			

Advisors

(List name, address and home telephone for each person)

	Full Name	Address	Telephone Number
Lawyer			
Accountant			
Financial Advisor			
Stockbroker			
Insurance Agent			
Other Information:			

Document Locations

Description	Location	Other Information
Last Will & Testament		
Trust Agreement		
Living Will		
Healthcare Power of Attorney		
Power of Attorney for Finance and Property		
Title Deeds		
Leases		
Share Certificates		
Mortgage Documents		
Birth Certificate		
Marriage Certificate		

Divorce Decree		
Donor Cards		
Other Documents		

Funeral Plan

(Describe in general terms what funeral and burial arrangements you would like to have)

APPENDIX 3

SAMPLE WILLS

Appendix 3

APPENDIX 3

SAMPLE WILLS

First Will & Second Will – unmarried and not in a registered domestic partnership, with no children

These are "Simple Wills" and are used where a person is unmarried, and not in a registered domestic partnership and does not have any children. The Will is used to appoint an executor and to pass your estate to designated persons of your choice.

The First Will should be used where you have one intended beneficiary for the residue of your estate.

The Second Will should be used where you have more than one intended beneficiary for the residue of your estate.

Third Will – unmarried and not in a registered domestic partnership, with children

This will is for use by a person who is unmarried, not in a registered domestic partnership and has children. A trust will be created for the benefit of your children with power for the trustees to provide for your children until they reach a specific age (usually 18 to 21 years). Thereafter the residuary of your estate will be divided equally between your children.

Fourth Will & Fifth Will – married or in a registered domestic partnership with adult children

These wills are for use by couples who are married or in a registered domestic partnership with adult children. In these wills, each spouse/partner leaves their estate to the other with a provision that, should the surviving spouse/partner die within a period of 30 days of the other spouse/partner, the entire estate will pass to a different named beneficiary.

The Fourth Will is for use by a husband or male partner. The Fifth Will is for use by a wife or female partner.

Sixth Will & Seventh Will – married or in a registered domestic partnership with minor children

These wills are for use by couples who are married or in a registered domestic partnership with minor children. In these wills, each spouse/partner leaves their estate to the other with a provision that, should they both die within a period of 30 days of each other the entire estate will pass to the trustees of the estate to hold same on trust for the benefit of their minor children.

The Sixth Will is for use by a husband or male partner. The Seventh Will is for use by a wife or female partner.

Eight Will & Ninth Will – married or in a registered domestic partnership with no children

These are "Simple Wills" and are used where a person is married, or in a registered domestic partnership and does not have any children. The Will is used to appoint an executor and to pass your estate to designated persons of your choice.

The Eight Will should be used where you have one intended beneficiary for the residue of your estate.

The Ninth Will should be used where you have more than one intended beneficiary for the residue of your estate.

FIRST WILL

(Person who is not married and not in a registered domestic partnership and has no children, single beneficiary)

LAST WILL AND TESTAMENT

OF

_____

I, _____, of _____ in the State of _____, County of _____, being of sound and disposing mind and memory and having attained the age of majority in my state, hereby **REVOKE** all former wills, codicils and other testamentary dispositions at any time heretofore made by me and declare this to be my last will.

FIRST: I am not married nor do I have a registered domestic partner. I do not have any living children.

SECOND: I appoint _____ of _____ to be executor of this my will. If this person or institution shall for any reason be unable or unwilling to act (at any time) as my executor, then I appoint _____ of _____ to be the executor of my will. No executor appointed hereunder shall be required to post bond.

THIRD: I direct my executor to pay all my just debts (which are capable of enforcement against me), funeral and testamentary expenses as soon as practical after my death.

FOURTH: I give, devise, and bequeath _____ to _____ of _____ absolutely.

FIFTH: I give, devise, and bequeath _____ to

_____ of _____ absolutely.

[Repeat or delete as necessary to make further specific gifts/bequests. Note you may need to renumber subsequent clauses]

SIXTH: As to all the rest, residue and remainder of my estate of whatsoever nature and wheresoever situate I give devise and bequeath the same to _____ of ____ _____. However, in the event that this person predeceases me or refuses to accept this gift, then I give devise and bequeath all the rest, residue and remainder of my estate to _____ of _____ _____.

SEVENTH: In addition to all powers allowable to executors under the laws of this state, my executor shall have the following powers:

(a) to dispose of any property or any interest therein at such times and upon such terms and conditions as shall seem proper and to give good and sufficient instruments of transfer and to receive the proceeds of any such disposition;

(b) to purchase, manage, maintain and insure any property and to lease the same for such periods and on such terms as shall seem advantageous, and if advisable to pay for the value of any improvements made by a tenant under any such lease; to incur, extend or renew mortgage indebtedness; to make ordinary and extraordinary repairs and alterations to any building, to raze or erect buildings and to make improvements or to abandon any buildings or property; and to make any agreement of partition of such property and to give or receive money or other property in connection therewith;

(c) to exercise or sell all rights, options, powers and privileges, and to vote in person or by proxy, in relation to any stocks, bonds or other securities, all as fully as might be done by persons owning similar property in their own right;

(d) to manage, sell, administer, liquidate, continue or otherwise deal with any corporation, partnership or other business interest received by my trust estate as my executor deems fit;

(e) to institute, defend, settle or compromise, by arbitration or otherwise, all claims;

(f) to employ or retain such agents and advisors, including any firm with which any fiduciary may be affiliated, as may seem advisable and to delegate authority thereto, and to compensate them from the funds of my estate provided such compensation is reasonable in the circumstances;

(g) to settle any entitlement of any beneficiary, in part or in whole, by payment in cash or by the transfer of a specific asset or assets to the beneficiary or to the legal guardian of the beneficiary with power to require the beneficiary or any such guardian to accept such asset or assets at such value or estimate of value as my executor shall (acting reasonably) unilaterally deem fair; and

(h) to pay all necessary or proper expenses and charges from income or principal, or partly from each, in such manner as may seem equitable.

EIGHTH: To the extent that provision has not been made under the will for the management of any property, asset or item to be given outright to a person who is a minor, my executor may, without court approval, pay or transfer all or part of such property to a parent or guardian of that minor or that minor's estate, to a custodian under the Uniform Transfers to Minors Act, or may defer payment or transfer of such property until the minor reaches the age of majority, as defined by his or her state of residence. No bond shall be required for such payments.

NINTH: I declare that no executor of this will shall be liable for any loss not attributable to the executor's own dishonesty or to the willful commission by the executor of any act known to be a breach of the executor's duties and obligations as executor.

TENTH: If any person, whether or not related to me by blood or in any way, shall attempt, either directly or indirectly, to set aside the probate of my will or oppose or contest any of the provisions hereof, then any share or interest in my estate given to that person under my will shall be revoked and, in its stead, I give and bequeath the sum of one dollar ($1.00), only that, and no further interest whatever in my estate to such person.

IN WITNESS HEREOF, I sign the foregoing as my Last Will and Testament, do it willingly and as my free and voluntary act for the purpose herein expressed, this _____ day of _____ 20__.

_____

(Signed)

Signed by the above-named as and for his/her Last Will and Testament in our presence, each of us being present at the same time who at his/her request and in his/her presence and in the presence of each other have hereunto subscribed our names as witnesses.

We, the witnesses, sign our name to this document, and we declare under penalty of perjury, that the foregoing is true and correct, this _____ day of _____, 20__.

Name: _____

Signature: _____

Address: _____

_____

_____

_____

Name: _____

Signature: _____

Address: _____

_____

_____

_____

SECOND WILL

(Person who is not married and not in a registered domestic partnership and has no children, multiple beneficiaries)

LAST WILL AND TESTAMENT

OF

_____

I, _____, of _____ in the State of _____, County of _____, being of sound and disposing mind and memory and having attained the age of majority in my state, hereby **REVOKE** all former wills, codicils and other testamentary dispositions at any time heretofore made by me and declare this to be my last will.

FIRST: I am not married nor do I have a registered domestic partner. I do not have any living children.

SECOND: I appoint _____ of _____ to be executor of this my will. If this person or institution shall for any reason be unable or unwilling to act (at any time) as my executor, then I appoint _____ of _____ to be the executor of my will. No executor appointed hereunder shall be required to post bond.

THIRD: I direct my executor to pay all my just debts (which are capable of enforcement against me), funeral and testamentary expenses as soon as practical after my death.

FOURTH: I give, devise, and bequeath _____ to _____ of _____ absolutely.

FIFTH: I give, devise, and bequeath _____ to

_____ of _____ absolutely.

[Repeat or delete as necessary to make further specific gifts/bequests. Note you may need to renumber subsequent clauses]

SIXTH: I give, devise, and bequeath all the rest, residue and remainder of my estate to _____ of _____ _ and _____ of _____ in equal shares. However, in the event that either of the above persons predeceases me or refuses this gift, then I give, devise and bequeath their share of my estate to _____ of _____ _____.

SEVENTH: In addition to all powers allowable to executors under the laws of this state, my executor shall have the following powers:

(a) to dispose of any property or any interest therein at such times and upon such terms and conditions as shall seem proper and to give good and sufficient instruments of transfer and to receive the proceeds of any such disposition;

(b) to purchase, manage, maintain and insure any property and to lease the same for such periods and on such terms as shall seem advantageous, and if advisable to pay for the value of any improvements made by a tenant under any such lease; to incur, extend or renew mortgage indebtedness; to make ordinary and extraordinary repairs and alterations to any building, to raze or erect buildings and to make improvements or to abandon any buildings or property; and to make any agreement of partition of such property and to give or receive money or other property in connection therewith;

(c) to exercise or sell all rights, options, powers and privileges, and to vote in person or by proxy, in relation to any stocks, bonds or other securities, all as fully as might be done by persons owning similar property in their own right;

(d) to manage, sell, administer, liquidate, continue or otherwise deal with any corporation, partnership or other business interest received by my trust estate as my executor deems fit;

(e) to institute, defend, settle or compromise, by arbitration or otherwise, all claims;

(f) to employ or retain such agents and advisors, including any firm with which any fiduciary may be affiliated, as may seem advisable and to delegate authority thereto, and to compensate them from the funds of my estate provided such compensation is reasonable in the circumstances;

(g) to settle any entitlement of any beneficiary, in part or in whole, by payment in cash or by the transfer of a specific asset or assets to the beneficiary or to the legal guardian of the beneficiary with power to require the beneficiary or any such guardian to accept such asset or assets at such value or estimate of value as my executor shall (acting reasonably) unilaterally deem fair; and

(h) to pay all necessary or proper expenses and charges from income or principal, or partly from each, in such manner as may seem equitable.

EIGHTH: To the extent that provision has not been made under the will for the management of any property, asset or item to be given outright to a person who is a minor, my executor may, without court approval, pay or transfer all or part of such property to a parent or guardian of that minor or that minor's estate, to a custodian under the Uniform Transfers to Minors Act, or may defer payment or transfer of such property until the minor reaches the age of majority, as defined by his or her state of residence. No bond shall be required for such payments.

NINTH: I declare that no executor of this will shall be liable for any loss not attributable to the executor's own dishonesty or to the willful commission by the executor of any act known to be a breach of the executor's duties and obligations as executor.

TENTH: If any person, whether or not related to me by blood or in any way, shall attempt, either directly or indirectly, to set aside the probate of my will or oppose or contest any of the provisions hereof, then any share or interest in my estate given to that person under my will shall be revoked and, in its stead, I give and bequeath the sum of one dollar ($1.00), only that, and no further interest whatever in my estate to such person.

IN WITNESS HEREOF, I sign the foregoing as my Last Will and Testament, do it willingly and as my free and voluntary act for the purpose herein expressed, this _____ day of _____ 20__.

_____

(Signed)

Signed by the above-named as and for his/her Last Will and Testament in our presence, each of us being present at the same time who at his/her request and in his/her presence and in the presence of each other have hereunto subscribed our names as witnesses.

We, the witnesses, sign our name to this document, and we declare under penalty of perjury, that the foregoing is true and correct, this _____ day of _____, 20___.

Name: _____

Signature: _____

Address: _____

_____

_____

_____

Name: _____

Signature: _____

Address: _____

_____

_____

_____

THIRD WILL

(Person who is not married and not in a registered domestic partnership and has children)

LAST WILL AND TESTAMENT

OF

_____

I, _____, of _____ in the State of _____, County of _____, being of sound and disposing mind and memory and having attained the age of majority in my state, hereby **REVOKE** all former wills, codicils and other testamentary dispositions at any time heretofore made by me and declare this to be my last will.

FIRST: I am not married nor do I have a registered domestic partner. I have ____ child/ children namely _____.

SECOND: I appoint _____ of _____ to be executor and trustee of this my will (my "Trustee"). If this person or institution shall for any reason be unable or unwilling to act (at any time) as my Trustee, then I appoint _____ of _____ to be my Trustee. No Trustee appointed hereunder shall be required to post bond.

THIRD: I direct my Trustee to pay all my just debts (which are capable of enforcement against me), funeral and testamentary expenses as soon as practical after my death.

FOURTH: I appoint _____ of _____ and _____ of _____ guardians of my infant children and conservators of the estate of each of my infant children, to serve as such without bond.

FIFTH: I give, devise, and bequeath _____ to
_____ of _____ absolutely.

SIXTH: I give, devise, and bequeath _____ to
_____ of _____ absolutely.

[Repeat or delete as necessary to make further specific gifts/bequests. Note you may need to renumber subsequent clauses]

SEVENTH: I give, devise, and bequeath to my Trustee all the rest, residue and remainder of my estate upon trust to hold the same or the proceeds of sale thereof as trustee and to divide the same among such of my children as shall survive me and reach the age of _____ years and if more than one in equal shares absolutely BUT if any child of mine dies before me or before attaining a vested interest leaving a child or children then such child or children shall on reaching the age of _____ years take per stirpes the share which his/her parent would otherwise have taken and if more than one in equal shares absolutely.

EIGHTH: In addition to all powers allowable to executors under the laws of this state, my executor shall have the following powers:

(a) to dispose of any property or any interest therein at such times and upon such terms and conditions as shall seem proper and to give good and sufficient instruments of transfer and to receive the proceeds of any such disposition;

(b) to purchase, manage, maintain and insure any property and to lease the same for such periods and on such terms as shall seem advantageous, and if advisable to pay for the value of any improvements made by a tenant under any such lease; to incur, extend or renew mortgage indebtedness; to make ordinary and extraordinary repairs and alterations to any building, to raze or erect buildings and to make improvements or to abandon any buildings or property; and to make any agreement of partition of such property and to give or receive money or other property in connection therewith;

(c) to exercise or sell all rights, options, powers and privileges, and to vote in person or by proxy, in relation to any stocks, bonds or other securities, all as fully as might be done by persons owning similar property in their own right;

(d) to manage, sell, administer, liquidate, continue or otherwise deal with any corporation, partnership or other business interest received by my trust estate as my executor deems fit;

(e) to institute, defend, settle or compromise, by arbitration or otherwise, all claims;

(f) to employ or retain such agents and advisors, including any firm with which any fiduciary may be affiliated, as may seem advisable and to delegate authority thereto, and to compensate them from the funds of my estate provided such compensation is reasonable in the circumstances;

(g) to settle any entitlement of any beneficiary, in part or in whole, by payment in cash or by the transfer of a specific asset or assets to the beneficiary or to the legal guardian of the beneficiary with power to require the beneficiary or any such guardian to accept such asset or assets at such value or estimate of value as my executor shall (acting reasonably) unilaterally deem fair; and

(h) to pay all necessary or proper expenses and charges from income or principal, or partly from each, in such manner as may seem equitable.

NINTH: In addition to all statutory powers and common law powers of gratuitous trustees, and special powers herein conferred, my trustee shall have the fullest powers of investment, realization, administration, management and division of the trust estate or any part thereof as if that trustee was the beneficial owner thereof; and, in particular, without prejudice to the generality of the foregoing, that trustee shall have the powers set out hereinafter:

(a) to receive from any person, to retain and to invest and reinvest in any kind of property or investment;

(b) to dispose of any property or any interest therein at such times and upon such terms and conditions as shall seem proper and to give good and sufficient instruments of transfer and to receive the proceeds of any such disposition;

(c) to purchase, manage, maintain and insure any property and to lease the same for such periods and on such terms as shall seem advantageous, and if advisable to pay for the value of any improvements made by a tenant under any such lease; to incur, extend or renew mortgage indebtedness; to make ordinary and extraordinary repairs and alterations to any building, to raze or erect buildings and to make improvements or to abandon any buildings or property; and to make any agreement of partition of such property and to give or receive money or other property in connection therewith;

(d) to exercise or sell all rights, options, powers and privileges, and to vote in person or by proxy, in relation to any stocks, bonds or other securities, all as fully as might be done by persons owning similar property in their own right;

(e) to assent to, oppose and participate in any reorganization, recapitalization, merger, consolidation or similar proceeding, to deposit securities, delegate discretionary powers, pay assessments or other expenses and exchange property, all as fully as might be done by persons owning similar property in their own right;

(f) to manage, sell, administer, liquidate, continue or otherwise deal with any corporation, partnership or other business interest received by my trust estate as the trustee deems fit;

(g) to borrow money and pledge or mortgage any property as security therefor;

(h) to institute, defend, settle or compromise, by arbitration or otherwise, all claims;

(i) to employ or retain such agents and advisors, including any firm with which any fiduciary may be affiliated, as may seem advisable and to delegate authority thereto, and to compensate them from the funds of my estate provided such compensation is reasonable in the circumstances; and

(j) to pay all necessary or proper expenses and charges from income or principal, or partly from each, in such manner as may seem equitable.

TENTH: To the extent that provision has not been made under the will for the management of any property, asset or item to be given outright to a person who is a minor, my executor may, without court approval, pay or transfer all or part of such property to a parent or guardian of that minor or that minor's estate, to a custodian under the Uniform Transfers to Minors Act, or may defer payment or transfer of such property until the minor reaches the age of majority, as defined by his or her state of residence. No bond shall be required for such payments.

ELEVENTH: I declare that any executor and/or trustee for the time being a lawyer or other person engaged in any profession or business shall be entitled to charge and be paid all usual professional or other reasonable and proper charges for business done or services rendered or time spent by him or his firm in proving this will and administering my estate and in relation to the trusts of this will or of any codicil to it whether in the ordinary course of his profession or business or not and although not of a nature requiring the employment of a lawyer or other professional or business person.

TWELVETH: I declare that income received after my death shall be treated as income of my estate regardless of the period to which it relates.

THIRTEENTH: I declare that no advancement shall be brought into account in the distribution of my estate.

FOURTEENTH: I declare that no executor of this will shall be liable for any loss not attributable to the executor's own dishonesty or to the willful commission by the executor of any act known to be a breach of executor's duties and obligations as executor.

FIFTEENTH: If any person, whether or not related to me by blood or in any way, shall attempt, either directly or indirectly, to set aside the probate of my will or oppose or contest any of the provisions hereof, then any share or interest in my estate given to that person under my will shall be revoked and, in its stead, I give and bequeath the sum of one dollar ($1.00), only that, and no further interest whatever in my estate to such person.

IN WITNESS HEREOF, I sign the foregoing as my Last Will and Testament, do it willingly and as my free and voluntary act for the purpose herein expressed, this _____ day of _____ 20__.

_____

(Signed)

Signed by the above-named as and for his/her Last Will and Testament in our presence, each of us being present at the same time who at his/her request and in his/her presence and in the presence of each other have hereunto subscribed our names as witnesses.

We, the witnesses, sign our name to this document, and we declare under penalty of perjury, that the foregoing is true and correct, this _____ day of _____, 20__.

Name: _____

Signature: _____

Address: _____

_____

_____

_____

Name: _____

Signature: _____

Address: _____

_____

_____

_____

FOURTH WILL

(Married or in a registered domestic partnership with adult children (for husband/male partner))

LAST WILL AND TESTAMENT

OF

_____

I, _____, of _____ in the State of _____, County of _____, being of sound and disposing mind and memory and having attained the age of majority in my state, hereby **REVOKE** all former wills, codicils and other testamentary dispositions at any time heretofore made by me and declare this to be my last will.

FIRST: [I am married to _____.]/[I am in a registered domestic partnership with_____.] I have _____ child/children namely _____.

SECOND: I appoint _____ of _____ to be executor of this my will. If this person or institution shall for any reason be unable or unwilling to act (at any time) as my executor, then I appoint _____ of _____ to be the executor of my will. No executor appointed hereunder shall be required to post bond.

THIRD: I direct my executor to pay all my just debts (which are capable of enforcement against me), funeral and testamentary expenses as soon as practical after my death.

FOURTH: I give, devise, and bequeath _____ to _____ of _____ absolutely.

FIFTH: I give, devise, and bequeath _____ to _____ of _____ absolutely.

[Repeat or delete as necessary to make further specific gifts/bequests. Note you may need to renumber subsequent clauses]

SIXTH: If my [spouse]/[partner], _____, shall survive me for a period of one month then **I GIVE, DEVISE AND BEQUEATH** all the rest, residue and remainder of my estate of whatsoever kind and wheresoever situate to my said [spouse]/[partner] absolutely.

SEVENTH: If my said [spouse]/[partner] shall predecease me or shall not survive me for the period aforesaid **I DIRECT** that the previous clause shall not take effect and this my will shall be construed and take effect as if the previous clause had been wholly omitted therefrom and that the remaining clauses of this will shall take effect.

EIGHTH: In so far as it may be necessary and for the avoidance of doubt I direct that if my [spouse]/[partner] shall survive me for a period of less than one month then the income of my estate accruing from the date of my death until the date of the death of my [spouse]/[partner] shall be accumulated and form part of my residuary estate.

NINTH: I give, devise, and bequeath all the rest, residue and remainder of my estate to _____ of _____ _ and _____ of _____ in equal shares. However, in the event that either of the above persons predeceases me or refuses this gift, then I give, devise and bequeath their share of my estate to _____ of _____ _____.

TENTH: In addition to all powers allowable to executors under the laws of this state, my executor shall have the following powers:

(a) to dispose of any property or any interest therein at such times and upon such terms and conditions as shall seem proper and to give good and sufficient instruments of transfer and to receive the proceeds of any such disposition;

(b) to purchase, manage, maintain and insure any property and to lease the same for such periods and on such terms as shall seem advantageous, and if advisable to pay for the value of any improvements made by a tenant under any such lease; to incur, extend or renew mortgage indebtedness; to make ordinary and extraordinary repairs and alterations to any building, to raze or erect buildings and to make improvements or to abandon any buildings or property; and to make any agreement of partition of such property and to give or receive money or other property in connection therewith;

(c) to exercise or sell all rights, options, powers and privileges, and to vote in person or by proxy, in relation to any stocks, bonds or other securities, all as fully as might be done by

persons owning similar property in their own right;

(d) to manage, sell, administer, liquidate, continue or otherwise deal with any corporation, partnership or other business interest received by my trust estate as my executor deems fit;

(e) to institute, defend, settle or compromise, by arbitration or otherwise, all claims;

(f) to employ or retain such agents and advisors, including any firm with which any fiduciary may be affiliated, as may seem advisable and to delegate authority thereto, and to compensate them from the funds of my estate provided such compensation is reasonable in the circumstances;

(g) to settle any entitlement of any beneficiary, in part or in whole, by payment in cash or by the transfer of a specific asset or assets to the beneficiary or to the legal guardian of the beneficiary with power to require the beneficiary or any such guardian to accept such asset or assets at such value or estimate of value as my executor shall (acting reasonably) unilaterally deem fair; and

(h) to pay all necessary or proper expenses and charges from income or principal, or partly from each, in such manner as may seem equitable.

ELEVENTH: To the extent that provision has not been made under the will for the management of any property, asset or item to be given outright to a person who is a minor, my executor may, without court approval, pay or transfer all or part of such property to a parent or guardian of that minor or that minor's estate, to a custodian under the Uniform Transfers to Minors Act, or may defer payment or transfer of such property until the minor reaches the age of majority, as defined by his or her state of residence. No bond shall be required for such payments.

TWELVETH: I declare that any executor and/or trustee for the time being a lawyer or other person engaged in any profession or business shall be entitled to charge and be paid all usual professional or other reasonable and proper charges for business done or services rendered or time spent by him or his firm in proving this will and administering my estate and in relation to the trusts of the will or of any codicil to it whether in the ordinary course of his profession or business or not and although not of a nature requiring the employment of a lawyer or other professional or business person.

THIRTEENTH: I declare that income received after my death shall be treated as income of my estate regardless of the period to which it relates.

FOURTEENTH: I declare that no executor of this will shall be liable for any loss not

attributable to the executor's own dishonesty or to the willful commission by the executor of any act known to be a breach of the executor's duties and obligations as executor.

FIFTEENTH: If any person, whether or not related to me by blood or in any way, shall attempt, either directly or indirectly, to set aside the probate of my will or oppose or contest any of the provisions hereof, then any share or interest in my estate given to that person under my will shall be revoked and, in its stead, I give and bequeath the sum of one dollar ($1.00), only that, and no further interest whatever in my estate to such person.

IN WITNESS HEREOF, I sign the foregoing as my Last Will and Testament, do it willingly and as my free and voluntary act for the purpose herein expressed, this _____ day of _____ 20__.

_____

(Signed)

Signed by the above-named as and for his Last Will and Testament in our presence, each of us being present at the same time who at his request and in his presence and in the presence of each other have hereunto subscribed our names as witnesses.

We, the witnesses, sign our name to this document, and we declare under penalty of perjury, that the foregoing is true and correct, this _____ day of _____, 20__.

Name: _____

Signature: _____

Address: _____

_____

_____

_____

Name: _____

Signature: _____

Address: _____

_____

_____

_____

FIFTH WILL

(Married or in a registered domestic partnership with adult children (for wife/female partner))

LAST WILL AND TESTAMENT

OF

_____

I, _____, of _____ in the State of _____, County of _____, being of sound and disposing mind and memory and having attained the age of majority in my state, hereby **REVOKE** all former wills, codicils and other testamentary dispositions at any time heretofore made by me and declare this to be my last will.

FIRST: [I am married to _____.]/[I am in a registered domestic partnership with_____.] I have _____ child/children namely _____.

SECOND: I appoint _____ of _____ to be executor of this my will. If this person or institution shall for any reason be unable or unwilling to act (at any time) as my executor, then I appoint _____ of _____ to be the executor of my will. No executor appointed hereunder shall be required to post bond.

THIRD: I direct my executor to pay all my just debts (which are capable of enforcement against me), funeral and testamentary expenses as soon as practical after my death.

FOURTH: I give, devise, and bequeath _____ to _____ of _____ absolutely.

FIFTH: I give, devise, and bequeath _____ to _____ of _____ absolutely.

[Repeat or delete as necessary to make further specific gifts/bequests. Note you may need to renumber subsequent clauses]

SIXTH: If my [spouse]/[partner], _____, shall survive me for a period of one month then **I GIVE, DEVISE AND BEQUEATH** all the rest, residue and remainder of my estate of whatsoever kind and wheresoever situate to my said [spouse]/[partner] absolutely.

SEVENTH: If my said [spouse]/[partner] shall predecease me or shall not survive me for the period aforesaid **I DIRECT** that the previous clause shall not take effect and this my will shall be construed and take effect as if the previous clause had been wholly omitted therefrom and that the remaining clauses of this will shall take effect.

EIGHTH: In so far as it may be necessary and for the avoidance of doubt I direct that if my [spouse]/[partner] shall survive me for a period of less than one month then the income of my estate accruing from the date of my death until the date of the death of my [spouse]/[partner] shall be accumulated and form part of my residuary estate.

NINTH: I give, devise, and bequeath all the rest, residue and remainder of my estate to _____ of _____
_ and _____ of _____ in equal shares. However, in the event that either of the above persons predeceases me or refuses this gift, then I give, devise and bequeath their share of my estate to _____ of _____
_____.

TENTH: In addition to all powers allowable to executors under the laws of this state, my executor shall have the following powers:

(a) to dispose of any property or any interest therein at such times and upon such terms and conditions as shall seem proper and to give good and sufficient instruments of transfer and to receive the proceeds of any such disposition;

(b) to purchase, manage, maintain and insure any property and to lease the same for such periods and on such terms as shall seem advantageous, and if advisable to pay for the value of any improvements made by a tenant under any such lease; to incur, extend or renew mortgage indebtedness; to make ordinary and extraordinary repairs and alterations to any building, to raze or erect buildings and to make improvements or to abandon any buildings or property; and to make any agreement of partition of such property and to give or receive money or other property in connection therewith;

(c) to exercise or sell all rights, options, powers and privileges, and to vote in person or by proxy, in relation to any stocks, bonds or other securities, all as fully as might be done by

persons owning similar property in their own right;

(d) to manage, sell, administer, liquidate, continue or otherwise deal with any corporation, partnership or other business interest received by my trust estate as my executor deems fit;

(e) to institute, defend, settle or compromise, by arbitration or otherwise, all claims;

(f) to employ or retain such agents and advisors, including any firm with which any fiduciary may be affiliated, as may seem advisable and to delegate authority thereto, and to compensate them from the funds of my estate provided such compensation is reasonable in the circumstances;

(g) to settle any entitlement of any beneficiary, in part or in whole, by payment in cash or by the transfer of a specific asset or assets to the beneficiary or to the legal guardian of the beneficiary with power to require the beneficiary or any such guardian to accept such asset or assets at such value or estimate of value as my executor shall (acting reasonably) unilaterally deem fair; and

(h) to pay all necessary or proper expenses and charges from income or principal, or partly from each, in such manner as may seem equitable.

ELEVENTH: To the extent that provision has not been made under the will for the management of any property, asset or item to be given outright to a person who is a minor, my executor may, without court approval, pay or transfer all or part of such property to a parent or guardian of that minor or that minor's estate, to a custodian under the Uniform Transfers to Minors Act, or may defer payment or transfer of such property until the minor reaches the age of majority, as defined by his or her state of residence. No bond shall be required for such payments.

TWELVETH: I declare that any executor and/or trustee for the time being a lawyer or other person engaged in any profession or business shall be entitled to charge and be paid all usual professional or other reasonable and proper charges for business done or services rendered or time spent by him or his firm in proving this will and administering my estate and in relation to the trusts of the will or of any codicil to it whether in the ordinary course of his profession or business or not and although not of a nature requiring the employment of a lawyer or other professional or business person.

THIRTEENTH: I declare that income received after my death shall be treated as income of my estate regardless of the period to which it relates.

FOURTEENTH: I declare that no executor of this will shall be liable for any loss not

attributable to the executor's own dishonesty or to the willful commission by the executor of any act known to be a breach of the executor's duties and obligations as executor.

FIFTEENTH: If any person, whether or not related to me by blood or in any way, shall attempt, either directly or indirectly, to set aside the probate of my will or oppose or contest any of the provisions hereof, then any share or interest in my estate given to that person under my will shall be revoked and, in its stead, I give and bequeath the sum of one dollar ($1.00), only that, and no further interest whatever in my estate to such person.

IN WITNESS HEREOF, I sign the foregoing as my Last Will and Testament, do it willingly and as my free and voluntary act for the purpose herein expressed, this _____ day of _____ 20__.

_____

(Signed)

Signed by the above-named as and for her Last Will and Testament in our presence, each of us being present at the same time who at her request and in her presence and in the presence of each other have hereunto subscribed our names as witnesses.

We, the witnesses, sign our name to this document, and we declare under penalty of perjury, that the foregoing is true and correct, this _____ day of _____, 20__.

Name: _____

Signature: _____

Address: _____

_____

_____

_____

Name: _____

Signature: _____

Address: _____

_____

_____

_____

SIXTH WILL

(Married or in a registered domestic partnership with minor children (for husband/male partner))

LAST WILL AND TESTAMENT

OF

_____

I, _____, of _____ in the State of _____, County of _____, being of sound and disposing mind and memory and having attained the age of majority in my state, hereby **REVOKE** all former wills, codicils and other testamentary dispositions at any time heretofore made by me and declare this to be my last will.

FIRST: [I am married to _____.]/[I am in a registered domestic partnership with_____.] I have _____ child/children namely _____.

SECOND: I appoint _____ of _____ to be executor and trustee of this my will (my "Trustee"). If this person or institution shall for any reason be unable or unwilling to act (at any time) as my Trustee, then I appoint _____ of _____ to be my Trustee. No Trustee appointed hereunder shall be required to post bond.

THIRD: I direct my Trustee to pay all my just debts (which are capable of enforcement against me), funeral and testamentary expenses as soon as practical after my death.

FOURTH: I appoint _____ of _____ and _____ of _____ guardians of my infant children and conservators of the estate of each of my infant children, to serve as such without bond.

FIFTH: I give, devise, and bequeath _____ to
_____ of _____ absolutely.

SIXTH: I give, devise, and bequeath _____ to
_____ of _____ absolutely.

[Repeat or delete as necessary to make further specific gifts/bequests. Note you may need to renumber subsequent clauses]

SEVENTH: If my [spouse]/[partner], _____, shall survive me for a period of one month then **I GIVE, DEVISE AND BEQUEATH** all the rest, residue and remainder of my estate of whatsoever kind and wheresoever situate to my said [spouse]/[partner] absolutely.

EIGHTH: If my said [spouse]/[partner] shall predecease me or shall not survive me for the period aforesaid **I DIRECT** that the previous clause shall not take effect and this my will shall be construed and take effect as if the previous clause had been wholly omitted therefrom and that the remaining clauses of this will shall take effect.

NINTH: In so far as it may be necessary and for the avoidance of doubt I direct that if my [spouse]/[partner] shall survive me for a period of less than one month then the income of my estate accruing from the date of my death until the date of the death of my [wife]/[partner] shall be accumulated and form part of my residuary estate.

TENTH: I give, devise, and bequeath to my Trustee all the rest, residue and remainder of my estate upon trust to hold the same or the proceeds of sale thereof as trustee and to divide the same among such of my children as shall survive me and reach the age of _____ years and if more than one in equal shares absolutely BUT if any child of mine dies before me or before attaining a vested interest leaving a child or children then such child or children shall on reaching the age of _____ years take per stirpes the share which his/her parent would otherwise have taken and if more than one in equal shares absolutely.

ELEVENTH: In addition to all powers allowable to executors under the laws of this state, my executor shall have the following powers:

(a) to dispose of any property or any interest therein at such times and upon such terms and conditions as shall seem proper and to give good and sufficient instruments of transfer and to receive the proceeds of any such disposition;

(b) to purchase, manage, maintain and insure any property and to lease the same for such periods and on such terms as shall seem advantageous, and if advisable to pay for the value of any improvements made by a tenant under any such lease; to incur, extend or renew mortgage indebtedness; to make ordinary and extraordinary repairs and alterations to any building, to raze or erect buildings and to make improvements or to abandon any buildings or property; and to make any agreement of partition of such property and to give or receive money or other property in connection therewith;

(c) to exercise or sell all rights, options, powers and privileges, and to vote in person or by proxy, in relation to any stocks, bonds or other securities, all as fully as might be done by persons owning similar property in their own right;

(d) to manage, sell, administer, liquidate, continue or otherwise deal with any corporation, partnership or other business interest received by my trust estate as my executor deems fit;

(e) to institute, defend, settle or compromise, by arbitration or otherwise, all claims;

(f) to employ or retain such agents and advisors, including any firm with which any fiduciary may be affiliated, as may seem advisable and to delegate authority thereto, and to compensate them from the funds of my estate provided such compensation is reasonable in the circumstances;

(g) to settle any entitlement of any beneficiary, in part or in whole, by payment in cash or by the transfer of a specific asset or assets to the beneficiary or to the legal guardian of the beneficiary with power to require the beneficiary or any such guardian to accept such asset or assets at such value or estimate of value as my executor shall (acting reasonably) unilaterally deem fair; and

(h) to pay all necessary or proper expenses and charges from income or principal, or partly from each, in such manner as may seem equitable.

TWELFTH: In addition to all statutory powers and common law powers of gratuitous trustees, and special powers herein conferred, my trustee shall have the fullest powers of investment, realization, administration, management and division of the trust estate or any part thereof as if that trustee was the beneficial owner thereof; and, in particular, without prejudice to the generality of the foregoing, that trustee shall have the powers set out hereinafter:

(a) to receive from any person, to retain and to invest and reinvest in any kind of property or investment;

(b) to dispose of any property or any interest therein at such times and upon such terms and conditions as shall seem proper and to give good and sufficient instruments of transfer and to receive the proceeds of any such disposition;

(c)   to purchase, manage, maintain and insure any property and to lease the same for such periods and on such terms as shall seem advantageous, and if advisable to pay for the value of any improvements made by a tenant under any such lease; to incur, extend or renew mortgage indebtedness; to make ordinary and extraordinary repairs and alterations to any building, to raze or erect buildings and to make improvements or to abandon any buildings or property; and to make any agreement of partition of such property and to give or receive money or other property in connection therewith;

(d)   to exercise or sell all rights, options, powers and privileges, and to vote in person or by proxy, in relation to any stocks, bonds or other securities, all as fully as might be done by persons owning similar property in their own right;

(e)   to assent to, oppose and participate in any reorganization, recapitalization, merger, consolidation or similar proceeding, to deposit securities, delegate discretionary powers, pay assessments or other expenses and exchange property, all as fully as might be done by persons owning similar property in their own right;

(f)   to manage, sell, administer, liquidate, continue or otherwise deal with any corporation, partnership or other business interest received by my trust estate as the trustee deems fit;

(g)   to borrow money and pledge or mortgage any property as security therefor;

(h)   to institute, defend, settle or compromise, by arbitration or otherwise, all claims;

(i)   to employ or retain such agents and advisors, including any firm with which any fiduciary may be affiliated, as may seem advisable and to delegate authority thereto, and to compensate them from the funds of my estate provided such compensation is reasonable in the circumstances; and

(j)   to pay all necessary or proper expenses and charges from income or principal, or partly from each, in such manner as may seem equitable.

THIRTEENTH: To the extent that provision has not been made under the will for the management of any property, asset or item to be given outright to a person who is a minor, my executor may, without court approval, pay or transfer all or part of such property to a parent or guardian of that minor or that minor's estate, to a custodian under the Uniform Transfers to Minors Act, or may defer payment or transfer of such property until the minor reaches the age of majority, as defined by his or her state of residence. No bond shall be required for such payments.

FOURTEENTH: I declare that any executor and/or trustee for the time being a lawyer or other person engaged in any profession or business shall be entitled to charge and be paid all usual professional or other reasonable and proper charges for business done or services rendered or time spent by him or his firm in proving this will and administering my estate and in relation to the trusts of the will or of any codicil to it whether in the ordinary course of his profession or business or not and although not of a nature requiring the employment of a lawyer or other professional or business person.

FIFTEENTH: I declare that income received after my death shall be treated as income of my estate regardless of the period to which it relates.

SIXTEENTH: I declare that no advancement shall be brought into account in the distribution of my estate.

SEVENTEENTH: I declare that no executor of this will shall be liable for any loss not attributable to the executor's own dishonesty or to the willful commission by the executor of any act known to be a breach of the executor's duties and obligations as executor.

EIGHTEENTH: If any person, whether or not related to me by blood or in any way, shall attempt, either directly or indirectly, to set aside the probate of my will or oppose or contest any of the provisions hereof, then any share or interest in my estate given to that person under my will shall be revoked and, in its stead, I give and bequeath the sum of one dollar ($1.00), only that, and no further interest whatever in my estate to such person.

_____

(Signed)

Signed by the above-named as and for his Last Will and Testament in our presence, each of us being present at the same time who at his request and in his presence and in the presence of each other have hereunto subscribed our names as witnesses.

We, the witnesses, sign our name to this document, and we declare under penalty of perjury, that the foregoing is true and correct, this _____ day of _____, 20__.

Name: _____

Signature: _____

Address: _____

_____

_____

_____

Name: _____

Signature: _____

Address: _____

_____

_____

_____

SEVENTH WILL

(Married or in a registered domestic partnership with minor children (for wife/female partner))

LAST WILL AND TESTAMENT

OF

_____

I, _____, of _____ in the State of _____, County of _____, being of sound and disposing mind and memory and having attained the age of majority in my state, hereby **REVOKE** all former wills, codicils and other testamentary dispositions at any time heretofore made by me and declare this to be my last will.

FIRST: [I am married to _____.]/[I am in a registered domestic partnership with_____.] I have _____ child/children namely _____.

SECOND: I appoint _____ of _____ to be executor and trustee of this my will (my "Trustee"). If this person or institution shall for any reason be unable or unwilling to act (at any time) as my Trustee, then I appoint _____ of _____ to be my Trustee. No Trustee appointed hereunder shall be required to post bond.

THIRD: I direct my Trustee to pay all my just debts (which are capable of enforcement against me), funeral and testamentary expenses as soon as practical after my death.

FOURTH: I appoint _____ of _____ and _____ of _____ guardians of my infant children and conservators of the estate of each of my infant children, to serve as such without bond.

FIFTH: I give, devise, and bequeath _____ to _____ of _____ absolutely.

SIXTH: I give, devise, and bequeath _____ to _____ of _____ absolutely.

[Repeat or delete as necessary to make further specific gifts/ bequests. Note you may need to renumber subsequent clauses]

SEVENTH: If my [spouse]/[partner], _____, shall survive me for a period of one month then **I GIVE, DEVISE AND BEQUEATH** all the rest, residue and remainder of my estate of whatsoever kind and wheresoever situate to my said [spouse]/ [partner] absolutely.

EIGHTH: If my said [spouse]/[partner] shall predecease me or shall not survive me for the period aforesaid **I DIRECT** that the previous clause shall not take effect and this my will shall be construed and take effect as if the previous clause had been wholly omitted therefrom and that the remaining clauses of this will shall take effect.

NINTH: In so far as it may be necessary and for the avoidance of doubt I direct that if my [spouse]/[partner] shall survive me for a period of less than one month then the income of my estate accruing from the date of my death until the date of the death of my [spouse]/[partner] shall be accumulated and form part of my residuary estate.

TENTH: I give, devise, and bequeath to my Trustee all the rest, residue and remainder of my estate upon trust to hold the same or the proceeds of sale thereof as trustee and to divide the same among such of my children as shall survive me and reach the age of _____ years and if more than one in equal shares absolutely BUT if any child of mine dies before me or before attaining a vested interest leaving a child or children then such child or children shall on reaching the age of _____ years take per stirpes the share which his/her parent would otherwise have taken and if more than one in equal shares absolutely.

ELEVENTH: In addition to all powers allowable to executors under the laws of this state, my executor shall have the following powers:

(a) to dispose of any property or any interest therein at such times and upon such terms and conditions as shall seem proper and to give good and sufficient instruments of transfer and to receive the proceeds of any such disposition;

(b) to purchase, manage, maintain and insure any property and to lease the same for such periods and on such terms as shall seem advantageous, and if advisable to pay for the value of any improvements made by a tenant under any such lease; to incur, extend or renew mortgage indebtedness; to make ordinary and extraordinary repairs and alterations to any building, to raze or erect buildings and to make improvements or to abandon any buildings or property; and to make any agreement of partition of such property and to give or receive money or other property in connection therewith;

(c) to exercise or sell all rights, options, powers and privileges, and to vote in person or by proxy, in relation to any stocks, bonds or other securities, all as fully as might be done by persons owning similar property in their own right;

(d) to manage, sell, administer, liquidate, continue or otherwise deal with any corporation, partnership or other business interest received by my trust estate as my executor deems fit;

(e) to institute, defend, settle or compromise, by arbitration or otherwise, all claims;

(f) to employ or retain such agents and advisors, including any firm with which any fiduciary may be affiliated, as may seem advisable and to delegate authority thereto, and to compensate them from the funds of my estate provided such compensation is reasonable in the circumstances;

(g) to settle any entitlement of any beneficiary, in part or in whole, by payment in cash or by the transfer of a specific asset or assets to the beneficiary or to the legal guardian of the beneficiary with power to require the beneficiary or any such guardian to accept such asset or assets at such value or estimate of value as my executor shall (acting reasonably) unilaterally deem fair; and

(h) to pay all necessary or proper expenses and charges from income or principal, or partly from each, in such manner as may seem equitable.

TWELFTH: In addition to all statutory powers and common law powers of gratuitous trustees, and special powers herein conferred, my trustee shall have the fullest powers of investment, realization, administration, management and division of the trust estate or any part thereof as if that trustee was the beneficial owner thereof; and, in particular, without prejudice to the generality of the foregoing, that trustee shall have the powers set out hereinafter:

(a) to receive from any person, to retain and to invest and reinvest in any kind of property or investment;

(b) to dispose of any property or any interest therein at such times and upon such terms and conditions as shall seem proper and to give good and sufficient instruments of transfer and to receive the proceeds of any such disposition;

(c) to purchase, manage, maintain and insure any property and to lease the same for such periods and on such terms as shall seem advantageous, and if advisable to pay for the value of any improvements made by a tenant under any such lease; to incur, extend or renew mortgage indebtedness; to make ordinary and extraordinary repairs and alterations to any building, to raze or erect buildings and to make improvements or to abandon any buildings or property; and to make any agreement of partition of such property and to give or receive money or other property in connection therewith;

(d) to exercise or sell all rights, options, powers and privileges, and to vote in person or by proxy, in relation to any stocks, bonds or other securities, all as fully as might be done by persons owning similar property in their own right;

(e) to assent to, oppose and participate in any reorganization, recapitalization, merger, consolidation or similar proceeding, to deposit securities, delegate discretionary powers, pay assessments or other expenses and exchange property, all as fully as might be done by persons owning similar property in their own right;

(f) to manage, sell, administer, liquidate, continue or otherwise deal with any corporation, partnership or other business interest received by my trust estate as the trustee deems fit;

(g) to borrow money and pledge or mortgage any property as security therefor;

(h) to institute, defend, settle or compromise, by arbitration or otherwise, all claims;

(i) to employ or retain such agents and advisors, including any firm with which any fiduciary may be affiliated, as may seem advisable and to delegate authority thereto, and to compensate them from the funds of my estate provided such compensation is reasonable in the circumstances; and

(j) to pay all necessary or proper expenses and charges from income or principal, or partly from each, in such manner as may seem equitable.

THIRTEENTH: To the extent that provision has not been made under the will for the management of any property, asset or item to be given outright to a person who is a minor, my executor may, without court approval, pay or transfer all or part of such property to a parent or guardian of that minor or that minor's estate, to a custodian under the Uniform Transfers to Minors Act, or may defer payment or transfer of such property until the minor reaches the age of majority, as defined by his or her state of residence. No bond shall be required for such payments.

FOURTEENTH: I declare that any executor and/or trustee for the time being a lawyer or other person engaged in any profession or business shall be entitled to charge and be paid all usual professional or other reasonable and proper charges for business done or services rendered or time spent by him or his firm in proving this will and administering my estate and in relation to the trusts of the will or of any codicil to it whether in the ordinary course of his profession or business or not and although not of a nature requiring the employment of a lawyer or other professional or business person.

FIFTEENTH: I declare that income received after my death shall be treated as income of my estate regardless of the period to which it relates.

SIXTEENTH: I declare that no advancement shall be brought into account in the distribution of my estate.

SEVENTEENTH: I declare that no executor of this will shall be liable for any loss not attributable to the executor's own dishonesty or to the willful commission by the executor of any act known to be a breach of the executor's duties and obligations as executor.

EIGHTEENTH: If any person, whether or not related to me by blood or in any way, shall attempt, either directly or indirectly, to set aside the probate of my will or oppose or contest any of the provisions hereof, then any share or interest in my estate given to that person under my will shall be revoked and, in its stead, I give and bequeath the sum of one dollar ($1.00), only that, and no further interest whatever in my estate to such person.

_____

(Signed)

Signed by the above-named as and for her Last Will and Testament in our presence, each of us being present at the same time who at her request and in her presence and in the presence of each other have hereunto subscribed our names as witnesses.

We, the witnesses, sign our name to this document, and we declare under penalty of perjury, that the foregoing is true and correct, this _____ day of _____, 20__.

Name: _____

Signature: _____

Address: _____

_____

_____

_____

Name: _____

Signature: _____

Address: _____

_____

_____

_____

EIGHT WILL

(Married or in a registered domestic partnership with no children (for husband/male partner))

LAST WILL AND TESTAMENT

OF

_____

I, _____, of _____ in the State of _____, County of _____, being of sound and disposing mind and memory and having attained the age of majority in my state, hereby **REVOKE** all former wills, codicils and other testamentary dispositions at any time heretofore made by me and declare this to be my last will.

FIRST: [I am married to _____.]/[I am in a registered domestic partnership with_____.] I do not have any living children.

SECOND: I appoint _____ of _____ to be executor of this my will. If this person or institution shall for any reason be unable or unwilling to act (at any time) as my executor, then I appoint _____ of _____ to be the executor of my will. No executor appointed hereunder shall be required to post bond.

THIRD: I direct my executor to pay all my just debts (which are capable of enforcement against me), funeral and testamentary expenses as soon as practical after my death.

FOURTH: I give, devise, and bequeath _____ to _____ of _____ absolutely.

FIFTH: I give, devise, and bequeath _____ to _____ of _____ absolutely.

[Repeat or delete as necessary to make further specific gifts/bequests. Note you may need to renumber subsequent clauses]

SIXTH: If my [wife]/[partner], _____, shall survive me for a period of one month then **I GIVE, DEVISE AND BEQUEATH** all the rest, residue and remainder of my estate of whatsoever kind and wheresoever situate to my said [wife]/[partner] absolutely.

SEVENTH: If my said [wife]/[partner] shall predecease me or shall not survive me for the period aforesaid **I DIRECT** that the previous clause shall not take effect and this my will shall be construed and take effect as if the previous clause had been wholly omitted therefrom and that the remaining clauses of this will shall take effect.

EIGHTH: In so far as it may be necessary and for the avoidance of doubt I direct that if my [wife]/[partner] shall survive me for a period of less than one month then the income of my estate accruing from the date of my death until the date of the death of my [wife]/[partner] shall be accumulated and form part of my residuary estate.

NINTH: I give, devise, and bequeath all the rest, residue and remainder of my estate to _____ of _____ _ and _____ of _____ in equal shares. However, in the event that either of the above persons predeceases me or refuses this gift, then I give, devise and bequeath their share of my estate to _____ of _____ _____.

TENTH: In addition to all powers allowable to executors under the laws of this state, my executor shall have the following powers:

(a) to dispose of any property or any interest therein at such times and upon such terms and conditions as shall seem proper and to give good and sufficient instruments of transfer and to receive the proceeds of any such disposition;

(b) to purchase, manage, maintain and insure any property and to lease the same for such periods and on such terms as shall seem advantageous, and if advisable to pay for the value of any improvements made by a tenant under any such lease; to incur, extend or renew mortgage indebtedness; to make ordinary and extraordinary repairs and alterations to any building, to raze or erect buildings and to make improvements or to abandon any buildings or property; and to make any agreement of partition of such property and to give or receive money or other property in connection therewith;

(c) to exercise or sell all rights, options, powers and privileges, and to vote in person or by proxy, in relation to any stocks, bonds or other securities, all as fully as might be done by

persons owning similar property in their own right;

(d) to manage, sell, administer, liquidate, continue or otherwise deal with any corporation, partnership or other business interest received by my trust estate as my executor deems fit;

(e) to institute, defend, settle or compromise, by arbitration or otherwise, all claims;

(f) to employ or retain such agents and advisors, including any firm with which any fiduciary may be affiliated, as may seem advisable and to delegate authority thereto, and to compensate them from the funds of my estate provided such compensation is reasonable in the circumstances;

(g) to settle any entitlement of any beneficiary, in part or in whole, by payment in cash or by the transfer of a specific asset or assets to the beneficiary or to the legal guardian of the beneficiary with power to require the beneficiary or any such guardian to accept such asset or assets at such value or estimate of value as my executor shall (acting reasonably) unilaterally deem fair; and

(h) to pay all necessary or proper expenses and charges from income or principal, or partly from each, in such manner as may seem equitable.

ELEVENTH: To the extent that provision has not been made under the will for the management of any property, asset or item to be given outright to a person who is a minor, my executor may, without court approval, pay or transfer all or part of such property to a parent or guardian of that minor or that minor's estate, to a custodian under the Uniform Transfers to Minors Act, or may defer payment or transfer of such property until the minor reaches the age of majority, as defined by his or her state of residence. No bond shall be required for such payments.

TWELVETH: I declare that any executor and/or trustee for the time being a lawyer or other person engaged in any profession or business shall be entitled to charge and be paid all usual professional or other reasonable and proper charges for business done or services rendered or time spent by him or his firm in proving this will and administering my estate and in relation to the trusts of the will or of any codicil to it whether in the ordinary course of his profession or business or not and although not of a nature requiring the employment of a lawyer or other professional or business person.

THIRTEENTH: I declare that income received after my death shall be treated as income of my estate regardless of the period to which it relates.

FOURTEENTH: I declare that no executor of this will shall be liable for any loss not

attributable to the executor's own dishonesty or to the willful commission by the executor of any act known to be a breach of the executor's duties and obligations as executor.

FIFTEENTH: If any person, whether or not related to me by blood or in any way, shall attempt, either directly or indirectly, to set aside the probate of my will or oppose or contest any of the provisions hereof, then any share or interest in my estate given to that person under my will shall be revoked and, in its stead, I give and bequeath the sum of one dollar ($1.00), only that, and no further interest whatever in my estate to such person.

IN WITNESS HEREOF, I sign the foregoing as my Last Will and Testament, do it willingly and as my free and voluntary act for the purpose herein expressed, this _____ day of _____ 20__.

_____

(Signed)

Signed by the above-named as and for his Last Will and Testament in our presence, each of us being present at the same time who at his request and in his presence and in the presence of each other have hereunto subscribed our names as witnesses.

We, the witnesses, sign our name to this document, and we declare under penalty of perjury, that the foregoing is true and correct, this _____ day of _____, 20__.

Name: _____

Signature: _____

Address: _____

_____

_____

_____

Name: _____

Signature: _____

Address: _____

_____

_____

_____

NINTH WILL

(Married or in a registered domestic partnership with no children (for wife/female partner))

LAST WILL AND TESTAMENT

OF

_____

I, _____, of _____ in the State of _____, County of _____, being of sound and disposing mind and memory and having attained the age of majority in my state, hereby **REVOKE** all former wills, codicils and other testamentary dispositions at any time heretofore made by me and declare this to be my last will.

FIRST: [I am married to _____.]/[I am in a registered domestic partnership with_____.] I do not have any living children.

SECOND: I appoint _____ of _____ to be executor of this my will. If this person or institution shall for any reason be unable or unwilling to act (at any time) as my executor, then I appoint _____ of _____ to be the executor of my will. No executor appointed hereunder shall be required to post bond.

THIRD: I direct my executor to pay all my just debts (which are capable of enforcement against me), funeral and testamentary expenses as soon as practical after my death.

FOURTH: I give, devise, and bequeath _____ to _____ of _____ absolutely.

FIFTH: I give, devise, and bequeath _____ to

_____ of _____ absolutely.

[Repeat or delete as necessary to make further specific gifts/bequests. Note you may need to renumber subsequent clauses]

SIXTH: If my [husband]/[partner], _____, shall survive me for a period of one month then **I GIVE, DEVISE AND BEQUEATH** all the rest, residue and remainder of my estate of whatsoever kind and wheresoever situate to my said [husband]/[partner] absolutely.

SEVENTH: If my said [husband]/[partner] shall predecease me or shall not survive me for the period aforesaid **I DIRECT** that the previous clause shall not take effect and this my will shall be construed and take effect as if the previous clause had been wholly omitted therefrom and that the remaining clauses of this will shall take effect.

EIGHTH: In so far as it may be necessary and for the avoidance of doubt I direct that if my [husband]/[partner] shall survive me for a period of less than one month then the income of my estate accruing from the date of my death until the date of the death of my [husband]/[partner] shall be accumulated and form part of my residuary estate.

NINTH: I give, devise, and bequeath all the rest, residue and remainder of my estate to _____ of _____ _ and _____ of _____ in equal shares. However, in the event that either of the above persons predeceases me or refuses this gift, then I give, devise and bequeath their share of my estate to _____ of _____ _____.

TENTH: In addition to all powers allowable to executors under the laws of this state, my executor shall have the following powers:

(a) to dispose of any property or any interest therein at such times and upon such terms and conditions as shall seem proper and to give good and sufficient instruments of transfer and to receive the proceeds of any such disposition;

(b) to purchase, manage, maintain and insure any property and to lease the same for such periods and on such terms as shall seem advantageous, and if advisable to pay for the value of any improvements made by a tenant under any such lease; to incur, extend or renew mortgage indebtedness; to make ordinary and extraordinary repairs and alterations to any building, to raze or erect buildings and to make improvements or to abandon any buildings or property; and to make any agreement of partition of such property and to give or receive money or other property in connection therewith;

(c) to exercise or sell all rights, options, powers and privileges, and to vote in person or by proxy, in relation to any stocks, bonds or other securities, all as fully as might be done by persons owning similar property in their own right;

(d) to manage, sell, administer, liquidate, continue or otherwise deal with any corporation, partnership or other business interest received by my trust estate as my executor deems fit;

(e) to institute, defend, settle or compromise, by arbitration or otherwise, all claims;

(f) to employ or retain such agents and advisors, including any firm with which any fiduciary may be affiliated, as may seem advisable and to delegate authority thereto, and to compensate them from the funds of my estate provided such compensation is reasonable in the circumstances;

(g) to settle any entitlement of any beneficiary, in part or in whole, by payment in cash or by the transfer of a specific asset or assets to the beneficiary or to the legal guardian of the beneficiary with power to require the beneficiary or any such guardian to accept such asset or assets at such value or estimate of value as my executor shall (acting reasonably) unilaterally deem fair; and

(h) to pay all necessary or proper expenses and charges from income or principal, or partly from each, in such manner as may seem equitable.

ELEVENTH: To the extent that provision has not been made under the will for the management of any property, asset or item to be given outright to a person who is a minor, my executor may, without court approval, pay or transfer all or part of such property to a parent or guardian of that minor or that minor's estate, to a custodian under the Uniform Transfers to Minors Act, or may defer payment or transfer of such property until the minor reaches the age of majority, as defined by his or her state of residence. No bond shall be required for such payments.

TWELVETH: I declare that any executor and/or trustee for the time being a lawyer or other person engaged in any profession or business shall be entitled to charge and be paid all usual professional or other reasonable and proper charges for business done or services rendered or time spent by him or his firm in proving this will and administering my estate and in relation to the trusts of the will or of any codicil to it whether in the ordinary course of his profession or business or not and although not of a nature requiring the employment of a lawyer or other professional or business person.

THIRTEENTH: I declare that income received after my death shall be treated as income of my estate regardless of the period to which it relates.

FOURTEENTH: I declare that no executor of this will shall be liable for any loss not attributable to the executor's own dishonesty or to the willful commission by the executor of any act known to be a breach of the executor's duties and obligations as executor.

FIFTEENTH: If any person, whether or not related to me by blood or in any way, shall attempt, either directly or indirectly, to set aside the probate of my will or oppose or contest any of the provisions hereof, then any share or interest in my estate given to that person under my will shall be revoked and, in its stead, I give and bequeath the sum of one dollar ($1.00), only that, and no further interest whatever in my estate to such person.

IN WITNESS HEREOF, I sign the foregoing as my Last Will and Testament, do it willingly and as my free and voluntary act for the purpose herein expressed, this _____ day of _____ 20__.

_____

(Signed)

Signed by the above-named as and for his Last Will and Testament in our presence, each of us being present at the same time who at his request and in his presence and in the presence of each other have hereunto subscribed our names as witnesses.

We, the witnesses, sign our name to this document, and we declare under penalty of perjury, that the foregoing is true and correct, this _____ day of _____, 20__.

Name: _____

Signature: _____

Address: _____

_____

_____

_____

Name: _____

Signature: _____

Address: _____

_____

_____

_____

APPENDIX 4

GENERAL INSTRUCTIONS FOR COMPLETING YOUR WILL

APPENDIX 4

GENERAL INSTRUCTIONS FOR COMPLETING YOUR WILL

1.   Carefully read all the instructions below and select the will from Appendix 3 which is most suitable to your circumstances.

2.   Carefully consider who will act as your executors, trustees, witnesses and guardians (if any). Carefully consider who will be the proposed beneficiaries. When inputting the details in your will, you must be as specific as possible and avoid broad statements such as "my friends".

3.   Print out the will form which you intend using and complete it neatly using a pen or carefully edit the text version of the form (that is available to you to download) on your computer.

        The will should be completed in accordance with the special instructions in Appendix 5 below.

        Do not leave any blank spaces.

4.   Arrange for your witnesses and you to meet with a Notary. ** Remember, in Vermont, you will need three witnesses instead of two!!

5.   Do not sign the will or the Affidavit (see Appendix 6 and Appendix 7) until you and the witnesses are with the Notary.

6.   Sign and date both the will and the Affidavit in the Notary's presence and have your witnesses do likewise.

7.   Have the Notary notarize the will and Affidavit.

NOTE In the event that you do not want to execute a self-proving affidavit, for whatever reason, you and your witnesses are free to execute the will otherwise than in the presence of a Notary. Again, only in the state of Louisiana must you have a will notarized. However, notarization is recommended for all states.

APPENDIX 5

SPECIFIC INSTRUCTIONS FOR COMPLETING YOUR WILL

APPENDIX 5

SPECIFIC INSTRUCTIONS FOR COMPLETING YOUR WILL

Instructions for completion of First Will document

1. Fill in your name in the space provided in the title "last will and testament of ____".

2. Fill in your name and address in the space provided in the first paragraph.

3. In the paragraph entitled "Second", fill in the name and address of your executor and the name and address of your alternate executor.**

4. In the paragraphs entitled "Fourth" and "Fifth", fill in the names and addresses of the proposed beneficiary of each specific gift and details of that specific gift. Add or delete gift clauses as you require but remember to re-number the subsequent clause numbers as appropriate.

5. In the paragraph entitled "Sixth", fill in the name and address of the sole beneficiary of your estate and the name and address of your alternate beneficiary.

6. Now Go To Number 4 in the General Instructions.

Instructions for completion of Second Will document

1. Fill in your name in the space provided in the title "last will and testament of ____".

2. Fill in your name and address in the space provided in the first paragraph.

3. In the paragraph entitled "Second", fill in the name and address of your executor and the name and address of your alternate executor.**

4. In the paragraphs entitled "Fourth" and "Fifth", fill in the names and addresses of the proposed beneficiary of each specific gift and details of that specific gift. Add or delete gift clauses as you require but remember to re-number the subsequent clause numbers as appropriate.

5. In the paragraph entitled "Sixth", fill in the name and address of the two beneficiaries

of your estate and the name and address of your alternate beneficiary. You can add more beneficiaries if you wish, but remember to state the percentage share of the residuary estate which they will be entitled to.

6.   Now Go To Number 4 in the General Instructions.

Instructions for completion of Third Will document

1.   Fill in your name in the space provided in the title "last will and testament of _____".

2.   Fill in your name and address in the space provided in the first paragraph.

3.   In the paragraph entitled "First", specify the number of children you have and the names of each child.

4.   In the paragraph entitled "Second", fill in the name and address of your executor and the name and address of your alternate executor.**

5.   In the paragraph entitled "Fourth", fill in the name and address of the each of the two proposed guardians of your minor children.

6.   In the paragraphs entitled "Fifth" and "Sixth", fill in the names and addresses of the proposed beneficiary of each specific gift and details of that specific gift. Add or delete gift clauses as you require but remember to re-number the subsequent clause numbers as appropriate.

7.   In the paragraph entitled "Seventh", fill in the age at which your children should receive their inheritance, for example, eighteen or twenty-one. This will need to be inserted in two places in this clause.

8.   Now Go To Number 4 in the General Instructions.

Instructions for completion of Fourth & Fifth Will documents

1.   Fill in your name in the space provided in the title "last will and testament of _____".

2.   Fill in your name and address in the space provided in the first paragraph.

3.   In the paragraph entitled "First", enter the name of your spouse or partner (and delete the section in square brackets regarding the spouse or partner which is not relevant to

your situation) and then specify the number of children you have and the names of each child. Remember to remove all square brackets.

4.   In the paragraph entitled "Second", fill in the name and address of your executor and the name and address of your alternate executor.**

5.   In the paragraphs entitled "Fourth" and "Fifth", fill in the names and addresses of the proposed beneficiary of each specific gift and details of that specific gift. Add or delete gift clauses as you require but remember to re-number the subsequent clause numbers as appropriate.

6.   In the paragraph entitled "Sixth", fill in the name of your spouse or partner and delete the part of the text "[spouse]/[partner]" which is not relevant to your situation – so that the text only reads either spouse or partner, as the case may be. You will need to make this deletion in two places in this clause. Remember to remove all square brackets.

7.   In the paragraph entitled "Seventh", delete the part of the text "[spouse]/[partner]" which is not relevant to your situation – so that the text only reads either spouse or partner, as the case may be. You will need to make this deletion in one place only in this clause. Remember to remove all square brackets.

8.   In the paragraph entitled "Eighth", delete the part of the text "[spouse]/[partner]" which is not relevant to your situation – so that the text only reads either spouse or partner, as the case may be. You will need to make this deletion in two places in this clause. Remember to remove all square brackets.

9.   In the paragraph entitled "Ninth", fill in the name and address of each of the beneficiaries of your estate who will benefit should your spouse or partner predecease you or fail to survive you by a period of one month.

10.   Now Go To Number 4 in the General Instructions.

Instructions for completion of Sixth and Seventh Will documents

1.   Fill in your name in the space provided in the title "last will and testament of _____".

2.   Fill in your name and address in the space provided in the first paragraph.

3.   In the paragraph entitled "First", enter the name of your spouse or partner (and delete the section in square brackets regarding the spouse or partner which is not relevant to

your situation) and then specify the number of children you have and the names of each child. Remember to remove all square brackets.

4. In the paragraph entitled "Second", fill in the name and address of your executor and the name and address of your alternate executor.**

5. In the paragraph entitled "Fourth", fill in the names and addresses of the proposed guardians of your infant children.

6. In the paragraphs entitled "Fifth" and "Sixth", fill in the names and addresses of the proposed beneficiary of each specific gift and details of that specific gift. Add or delete gift clauses as you require but remember to re-number the subsequent clause numbers as appropriate.

7. In the paragraph entitled "Seventh", fill in the name of your spouse or partner and delete the part of the text "[spouse]/[partner]" which is not relevant to your situation – so that the text only reads either spouse or partner, as the case may be. You will need to make this deletion in two places in this clause. Remember to remove all square brackets.

8. In the paragraph entitled "Eighth", delete the part of the text "[spouse]/[partner]" which is not relevant to your situation – so that the text only reads either spouse or partner, as the case may be. You will need to make this deletion in one place only in this clause. Remember to remove all square brackets.

9. In the paragraph entitled "Ninth", delete the part of the text "[spouse]/[partner]" which is not relevant to your situation – so that the text only reads either spouse or partner, as the case may be. You will need to make this deletion in two places in this clause. Remember to remove all square brackets.

10. In the paragraph entitled "Tenth", fill in the age at which your children should receive their inheritance, for example, eighteen or twenty-one. This will need to be entered in two places in this clause.

11. Now Go To Number 4 in the General Instructions.

Instructions for completion of Eight and Ninth Will document

1. Fill in your name in the space provided in the title "last will and testament of ____".

2. Fill in your name and address in the space provided in the first paragraph.

3.   In the paragraph entitled "First", enter the name of your spouse or partner (and delete the section in square brackets regarding the spouse or partner which is not relevant to your situation) and then specify the number of children you have and the names of each child. Remember to remove all square brackets.

4.   In the paragraph entitled "Second", fill in the name and address of your executor and the name and address of your alternate executor.**

5   In the paragraphs entitled "Fourth" and "Fifth", fill in the names and addresses of the proposed beneficiary of each specific gift and details of that specific gift. Add or delete gift clauses as you require but remember to re-number the subsequent clause numbers as appropriate.

6.   In the paragraph entitled "Sixth", fill in the name of your spouse or partner and delete the part of the text "[spouse]/[partner]" which is not relevant to your situation – so that the text only reads either spouse or partner, as the case may be. You will need to make this deletion in two places in this clause. Remember to remove all square brackets.

7.   In the paragraph entitled "Seventh", delete the part of the text "[spouse]/[partner]" which is not relevant to your situation – so that the text only reads either spouse or partner, as the case may be. You will need to make this deletion in one place only in this clause. Remember to remove all square brackets.

8.   In the paragraph entitled "Eighth", delete the part of the text "[spouse]/[partner]" which is not relevant to your situation – so that the text only reads either spouse or partner, as the case may be. You will need to make this deletion in two places in this clause. Remember to remove all square brackets.

9.   In the paragraph entitled "Ninth", fill in the name and address of each of the beneficiaries of your estate who will benefit should your spouse or partner predecease you or fail to survive you by a period of one month.

10.   Now Go To Number 4 in the General Instructions.

Note: Three Witnesses are required for wills executed in Vermont. In every other state, only two witnesses are required. Notarization is not required in any state other than Louisiana. You may need to amend your documents accordingly.

**Executors: Note, you may wish to appoint two executors (and two substitute executors) to act jointly. In this case, simply add the name and address of the second executor such that the sentence specifies that you appoint Person 1 and Person 2 to act as executors.

APPENDIX 6

SELF PROVING AFFIDAVIT - TYPE 1

FOR USE IN THE FOLLOWING STATES		
Alabama	Indiana	North Dakota
Alaska	Maine	Oregon
Arizona	Mississippi	South Carolina
Arkansas	Montana	South Dakota
Colorado	Nebraska	Tennessee
Hawaii	Nevada	Utah
Idaho	New Mexico	Washington
Illinois	New York	West Virginia

SELF-PROVING AFFIDAVIT

State of _____   **County of** _____

We,_____, _____

_____, and _____

_____, the testator and the witnesses respectively, whose names are signed to the attached instrument in those capacities, personally appearing before the undersigned authority and first being duly sworn, do hereby declare to the undersigned authority under penalty of perjury that the testator declared, signed, and executed the instrument as his/her last will; he/she signed it willingly or willingly directed another to sign for him/her; he/she executed it as his/her free and voluntary act for the purposes therein expressed; and each of the witnesses, at the request of the testator, in his or her hearing and presence, and in the presence of each other, signed the will as witness and that to the best of his or her knowledge the testator was at that time eighteen (18) years of age or older, of sound mind and under no constraint or undue influence.

_____ [Signature of Testator]
_____ [Printed or typed name of Testator]
_____ [Address of Testator, Line 1]
_____ [Address of Testator, Line 2]

_____ [Signature of Witness #1]
_____ [Printed or typed name of Witness #1]
_____ [Address of Witness #1, Line 1]
_____ [Address of Witness #1, Line 2]

_____ [Signature of Witness #2]
_____ [Printed or typed name of Witness #2]
_____ [Address of Witness #2, Line 1]
_____ [Address of Witness #2, Line 2]

Subscribed, sworn, and acknowledged before me, _____

_____, a notary public, by _____

_____, the testator, and by _____

_, and _____, the witnesses, this

_____ day of _____, 20_____.

[NOTARIAL SEAL]

_____

Notary Public's Signature

My Commission Expires: _____

APPENDIX 7

SELF PROVING AFFIDAVIT - TYPE 2

FOR USE IN THE FOLLOWING STATES		
Delaware	Kentucky	Oklahoma
Florida	Massachusetts	Pennsylvania
Georgia	Missouri	Rhode Island
Iowa	New Jersey	Virginia
Kansas	North Carolina	Wyoming

SELF-PROVING AFFIDAVIT

State of _____   **County of** _____

I, the undersigned, an officer authorized to administer oaths, certify that_____
_____, the testator, and _____, and
_____, the witnesses, whose names are signed to the attached
or foregoing instrument and whose signatures appear below, having appeared together before
me and having been first duly sworn, each then declare to me that the attached or foregoing
instrument is the last will of the testator; the testator willingly and voluntarily declared, signed
and executed the will or willingly directed another to sign in the presence of the witnesses;
the witnesses signed the will upon request by the testator, in the presence and hearing of the
testator, and in the presence of each other; to the best knowledge of each witness the testator
was, at the time of the signing, eighteen (18) years of age or older, of sound mind, and under no
constraint or undue influence; and each witness was and is competent, and of the proper age to
witness a will.

_____ [Signature of Testator]
_____ [Printed or typed name of Testator]
_____ [Address of Testator, Line 1]
_____ [Address of Testator, Line 2]

_____ [Signature of Witness #1]
_____ [Printed or typed name of Witness #1]
_____ [Address of Witness #1, Line 1]
_____ [Address of Witness #1, Line 2]

_____ [Signature of Witness #2]
_____ [Printed or typed name of Witness #2]
_____ [Address of Witness #2, Line 1]
_____ [Address of Witness #2, Line 2]

Subscribed, sworn, and acknowledged before me, _____
_____, a notary public, by _____
_____, the testator, and by _____

_, and _____, the witnesses, this _____ day of _____, 20_____.

SIGNED:

_____

_____

Official Capacity of Officer

APPENDIX 8

SELF PROVING AFFIDAVIT - TEXAS

SELF-PROVING AFFIDAVIT

THE STATE OF TEXAS   **COUNTY OF** _____

Before me, the undersigned authority, on this day personally appeared _____,
_____, and _____, known to me to be the testator and the wit-
nesses, respectively, whose names are subscribed to the annexed or foregoing instrument
in their respective capacities, and, all of said persons being by me duly sworn, the said
_____, testator, declared to me and to the said witnesses in my presence that
said instrument is his last will and testament, and that he had willingly made and executed it
as his free act and deed; and the said witnesses, each on his oath stated to me, in the presence and hearing of the said testator, that the said testator had declared to them that said
instrument is his last will and testament, and that he executed same as such and wanted each
of them to sign it as a witness; and upon their oaths each witness stated further that they did
sign the same as witnesses in the presence of the said testator and at his request; that he was
at that time eighteen years of age or over (or being under such age, was or had been lawfully
married, or was then a member of the armed forces of the United States or of an auxiliary
thereof or of the Maritime Service) and was of sound mind; and that each of said witnesses
was then at least fourteen years of age.

_____
Testator

_____
Witness

_____
Witness

Subscribed and sworn to before me by the said _____, testator, and by the
said _____ and _____, witnesses, this _____ day of
_____ A.D. _____.

(SEAL)

(Signed) _____
(Official Capacity of Officer)
Regards,

APPENDIX 9

ADDITIONAL CLAUSES YOU MAY WISH TO ADD

APPENDIX 9

ADDITIONAL CLAUSES THAT YOU MAY WISH TO ADD....

Appointing a custodian under UTMA

All property left under this Will to _____ [insert name of child], the management of which is not hereby otherwise provided for shall be given to _____ [insert name of primary custodian] of _____ [insert address of primary custodian], in the capacity of custodian under the _____ [insert state in which you are resident] Uniform Transfers to Minors Act, to hold until _____ [insert name of child] reaches _____ [insert age based on UTMA requirements] years of age. If _____ [insert name of custodian], is unwilling or unable to serve as custodian for any reason, then I appoint _____ [insert name of alternate custodian] of _____ [insert address of alternate custodian] to serve as custodian instead.

Appointing an alternate beneficiary for a specific gift

I give, devise, and bequeath _____ to _____ of _____ absolutely. If this person is unable or unwilling to accept this gift (for any reason) then I give same to _____ of _____ absolutely.

Releasing someone from a debt

I release and forgive _____ of _____ and should he/she predecease me his/her personal representatives and estate from all debt due to me at the date of my death and from all interest due in respect thereof.

Or

I release and forgive _____ of _____ and should he/she predecease me his/her personal representatives and estate from the debt of $_____ and from all interest due in respect thereof.

Nominating assets to be sold to pay taxes

I direct my executors to pay all estate, inheritance and succession taxes (including any interest and penalties thereon) payable by reason of my death using the following asset(s):-

_____.

Nominating assets to be sold to pay taxes

I direct my executors to pay my enforceable unsecured debts and funeral expenses, the expenses of my last illness, and the expenses of administering my estate using the following asset(s):-

_____.

Burial Clause

I direct that my executors should bury me at [*insert name and address of cemetery*].

Cremation Clause

I desire that my body be cremated in the crematorium at [*insert name and address of crematorium*]. I further direct that my ashes be [*insert details of what should be done with your ashes*].

APPENDIX 10

SOCIAL MEDIA ADDENDUM

SOCIAL MEDIA ADDENDUM
TO THE LAST WILL AND TESTAMENT

OF

_____

I, _____, of _____
_____ in the State of _____, County of
_____, executed my last will on [Date].
This addendum pertains solely to my social media and does not modify my will in any
other way. I hereby reaffirm my will in all respects other than as modified by this addendum. This codicil is specifically and solely intended to provide instructions on how to
deal with my social media upon my demise.

"Social media" for purposes of this codicil is intended to mean social networking sites,
online backup services, email accounts, photo and document sharing sites and blogs.
It does NOT include digital or virtual property items having monetary value, which I
may own the rights to. All digital or virtual property items of value are to be conveyed
pursuant to directions in my will and/or trust pertaining to "catch-all" or unidentified
property.

Included herewith as Schedule A is a listing of all of my social media accounts covered
and included by this addendum, and the logins and passwords to access the same. The
"digital executor" who I hereby direct and empower to access and deal with my social
media is:

I appoint _____ of _____ to be the digital
executor of this addendum. If this person or institution shall for any reason be unable
or unwilling to act (at any time) as my executor, then I appoint _____
of _____ to be the digital executor of this addendum.

My digital executor shall have the right and authority to manage, distribute or terminate
my social media without order of court and without notice. All specific or particular
instructions to my digital executor regarding how to do this are included in Schedule A.
Any matter not covered in said instructions is left to the prudence and judgment of my
digital executor. My digital executor shall receive no compensation for this service.

IN WITNESS HEREOF, I sign the foregoing as my Addendum to my Last Will and Testament, do it willingly and as my free and voluntary act for the purpose herein expressed, this _____ day of _____ 201__.

_____

(Signed)

Signed by the above-named as and for his/her Addendum in our presence, both of us being present at the same time who at his/her request and in his/her presence and in the presence of each other have hereunto subscribed our names as witnesses.

We, the witnesses, sign our name to this document, and we declare under penalty of perjury, that the foregoing is true and correct, this _____ day of _____, 20__.

Name: _____

Signature: _____

Address: _____

_____

_____

_____

Name: _____

Signature: _____

Address: _____

_____

_____

_____

Schedule A

Identification of Social Media and Instructions Regarding the Same:

Account: _____

Username/Password: _____

Instructions: _____

_____

_____

_____

_____

Account: _____

Username/Password: _____

Instructions: _____

_____

_____

_____

_____

Account: _____

Username/Password: _____

Instructions: _____

_____

_____

_____

_____

Account: _____

Username/Password: _____

Instructions: _____

_____

_____

_____

_____

Account: _____

Username/Password: _____

Instructions: _____

_____

_____

_____

Other Great Books from Enodare's Estate Planning Series

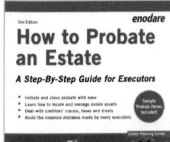

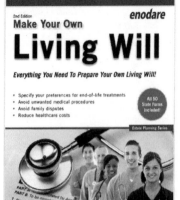

How to Probate an Estate - A Step-By-Step Guide for Executors

This book is essential reading for anyone contemplating acting as an executor of someone's estate!

Learn about the various stages of probate and what an executor needs to do at each stage to successfully navigate his way through to closing the estate and distributing the deceased's assets.

You will learn how an executor initiates probate, locates and manages assets, deals with debt and taxes, distributes assets, and much more. This is a fantastic step-by-step guide through the entire process!

Make Your Own Living Trust & Avoid Probate

Living trusts are used to distribute a person's assets after they die in a manner that avoids the costs, delays and publicity of probate. They also cater for the management of property during periods of incapacity.

This book will guide you step-by-step through the process of creating your very own living trust, transferring assets to your living trust and subsequently managing those assets.

All relevant forms are included.

Make Your Own Living Will

Do you want a say in what life sustaining medical treatments you receive during periods in which you are incapacitated and either in a permanent state of unconsciousness or suffering from a terminal illness? Well if so, you must have a living will!

This book will introduce you to living wills, the types of medical procedures that they cover, the matters that you need to consider when making them and, of course, provide you with all the relevant forms you need to make your own living will!

Other Great Books from Enodare's Estate Planning Series

Make Your Own Medical & Financial Powers of Attorney

Estate Planning Essentials

Funeral Planning Basics - A Step-By-Step Guide to Funeral Planning

The importance of having powers of attorney is often underappreciated. They allow people you trust to manage your property and financial affairs during periods in which you are incapacitated; as well as make medical decisions on your behalf based on the instructions in your power of attorney document. This ensures that your affairs don't go unmanaged and you don't receive any unwanted medical treatments.

This book provides all the necessary documents and step-by-step instructions to make a power of attorney to cover virtually any situation!

This book is a must read for anyone who doesn't already have a comprehensive estate plan.

It will show you the importance of having wills, trusts, powers of attorney and living wills in your estate plan. You will learn about the probate process, why people are so keen to avoid it and lots of simple methods you can actually use to do so. You will learn about reducing estate taxes and how best to provide for young beneficiaries and children.

This book is a great way to get you started on the way to making your own estate plan.

Through proper funeral planning, you can ensure that your loved ones are not confronted with the unnecessary burden of having to plan a funeral at a time which is already very traumatic for them.

This book will introduce you to issues such as organ donations, purchasing caskets, cremation, burial, purchasing grave plots, organization of funeral services, legal and financial issues, costs of pre-arranging a funeral, how to save money on funerals, how to finance funerals and much more.

Enodare's - Online Will Writer

Create Your Documents Online In Minutes

Enodare's secure Online Will Writer - Estate Planning Software enables you to immediately create, download and print documents such as wills, living trusts, living wills and powers of attorney from the comfort of your home and without delay! All documents are tailored in accordance with state laws!

Through the use of a simple question and answer process, we'll guide you step-by-step through the process of preparing your chosen document. It only takes a few minutes of your time and comprehensive help and information is available at every stage of the process. Of course you can always save you document and finish making it later; your information will remain secure. **Get Started Online Now!**

- ✔ **Save Time and Money**
- ✔ **Created by Experienced Attorneys**
- ✔ **Secured with 256 Bit Encryption**
- ✔ **100% Satisfaction Guarantee**

Note: The documents are valid in all states except Louisiana.

Over 10 Years Experience providing Online Wills and Trusts

Ensure Your Family's Protected

www.enodare.com

Developing an Effective Business Plan:
A Business Model Path to Success

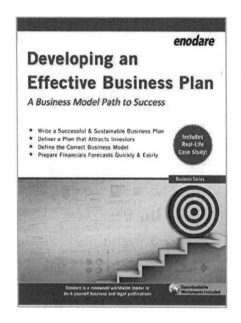

"Developing an Effective Business Plan: A Business Model Path to Success," will show you step-by-step how to use one of the most highly regarded business modeling techniques, the Business Model Canvas, to identify, test and validate the optimal business model for your enterprise. The book will then show you how to develop and write a business plan that will most effectively implement your validated business model.

Each component of an effective business model is addressed, both individually with its own dedicated chapter, and as a whole. Those components are: Market Segment; Value Proposition; Channels; Customer Relationships; Revenue Streams; Key Assets; Key Resources; Key Partnerships; and Cost Structure.

Then we turn to the business plan. You will learn how to write a compelling executive summary to attract investor interest; how to analyze and describe the business environment and market you will operate in; how to develop and describe your initial marketing plan, operations plan, e-commerce plan; and how to produce key financial projections that gauge your business's potential and serve as key benchmarks for future progress.

A detailed case study is used throughout the book to illustrate and help you understand how the process of creating a business model and writing a business plan plays out in the real world. By reading, studying and applying the techniques we discuss in this book, you will be able to lay a solid foundation for launching a successful and profitable business.

Personal Budget Kit

Budgeting Made Easy

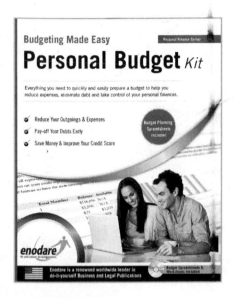

In this kit, we'll guide you step-by-step through the process of creating and living with a personal budget. We'll show you how analyze how you receive and spend your money and to set goals, both short and long-term.

You'll learn how to gain control of your personal cash flow. You'll discover when you need to make adjustments to your budget and how to do it wisely. Most of all, this kit will show you that budgeting isn't simply about adding limitations to your living but rather the foundation for living better by maximizing the resources you have.

This Personal Budget Kit provides you with step-by-step instructions, detailed information and all the budget worksheets and spreadsheets necessary to identify and understand your spending habits, reduce your expenses, set goals, prepare personal budgets, monitor your progress and take control over your finances.

- Reduce your spending painlessly and effortlessly

- Pay off your debts early

- Improve your credit rating

- Save & invest money

- Set & achieve financial goals

- Eliminate financial worries

Budget Planning Spreadsheets Included